Bristol before the Camera: The City in 1820-30

Watercolours and Drawings from the Braikenridge Collection

Sheena Stoddard

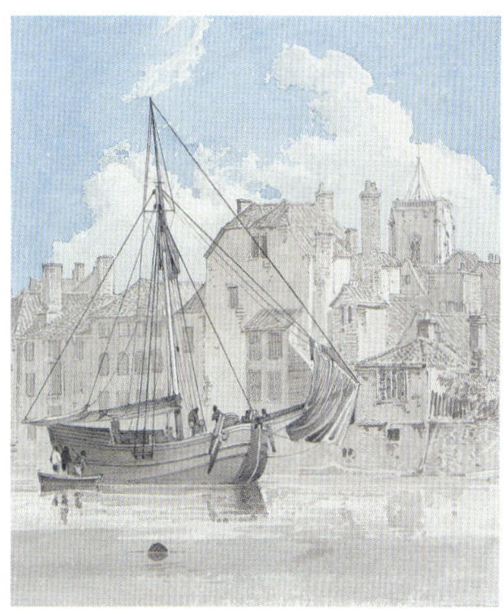

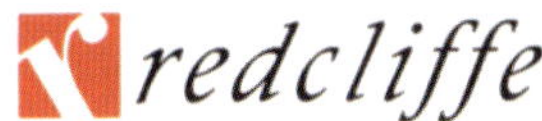

Redcliffe Press in association with Bristol Museums & Art Gallery

First published in 2001 by Redcliffe Press Ltd., 81g Pembroke Road, Bristol BS8 3EA
in association with Bristol Museums & Art Gallery
Telephone: 0117 9737207 Facsimile: 0117 9238991

ISBN 1 900178 68 0

British Library Cataloguing in Publication Data:
A catalogue record for this book is available from The British Library.

The publishers wish to thank The Friends of Bristol Art Gallery for their generous support of this publication.

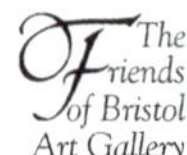

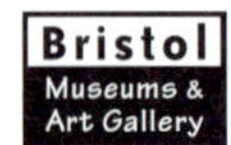

Acknowledgements

It would not have been possible to write this book without drawing on the knowledge of past and present colleagues at Bristol Museums & Art Gallery. The files in the Fine Art office have been built-up by curators over many years and contain a wealth of information. In addition, Andy Foyle and Stephen Price helped with matters architectural and Andy King with my maritime queries. My biggest thanks must go to John Bryant for his encyclopaedic knowledge of Bristol, which I have tapped intermittently for over fifteen years and excessively over the last few months. Andy Cotton took a large number of photographs in a short time.

Matthew Tanner, curator at ss *Great Britain*, was the only person who could solve the mystery of 'the dovecote at Wapping'. Christine Allen, a descendant of Thomas L Rowbotham, was generous in sharing her research.

A generous grant from The Friends of Bristol Art Gallery enabled the panoramas to be included.

Designed by Stephen Morris, Bristol and Liverpool (smc@freeuk.com), origination by Black Cat Graphics Bristol, and printed by Hackman Printers, Tonypandy, Rhondda.

Previous page:

Redcliffe waterfront with St Thomas' Church 1821
Hugh O'Neill

CONTENTS

1

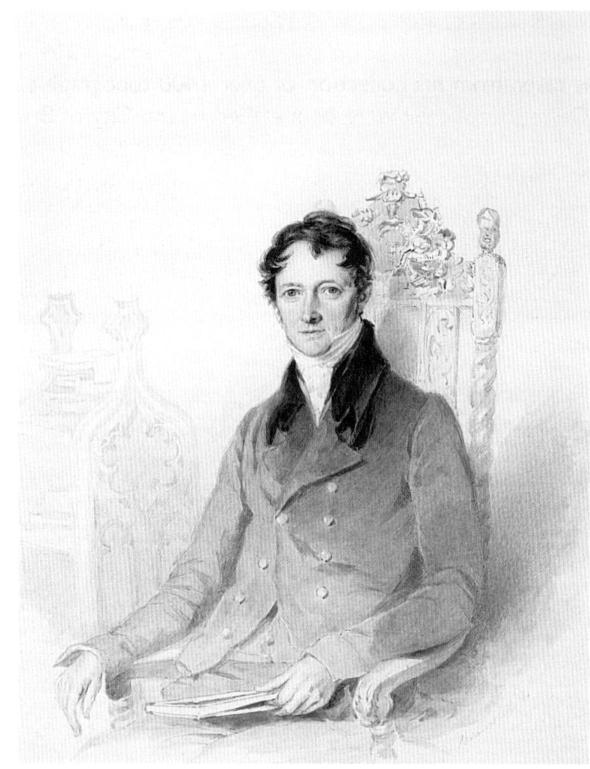

Portrait of George Weare Braikenridge c.1828

Nathan Cooper Branwhite

Braikenridge would have been in his early fifties when this portrait was drawn and a contemporary description said that he looked young for his age. He is sitting in a seventeenth-century walnut chair surmounted by the Stuart royal coat-of-arms. To his right is one of the pieces of hybrid furniture in his collection (furniture made-up of unrelated fragments of carving) with its ends formed by bench ends from an unknown church.

The artist, Nathan Cooper Branwhite (1775-1857), settled in Bristol about 1810 and lived in Queen Square. He was a miniature painter and portrait engraver who was known for achieving likenesses of his sitters. He also painted portraits in oil, and monochrome wash as here. The portrait has been dated on the basis of the costume and hair style of a companion drawing of Braikenridge's wife.

INTRODUCTION

Bristol is one of the best recorded cities prior to the invention of photography and we owe this to the foresight of one man, the collector and antiquary George Weare Braikenridge (1775-1856). This selection of about 100 drawings and watercolours is taken from his collection of over 1400 topographical views of Bristol. They have been in the care of Bristol Museums & Art Gallery since they were bequeathed to the City of Bristol by one of his sons in 1908. The selection of such a small proportion has inevitably resulted in the omission of many fine drawings and those chosen are largely views of the historic city and its harbour.

Braikenridge is remembered today for his Bristol collections but there was once much more. He collected widely and compulsively including stained glass, furniture, coins and medals, metalwork, illuminated manuscripts, autograph letters, ivory carvings, and wood-carvings in great abundance as well as any object – however humble – connected with Bristol's history. He was collecting the decorative arts when they were a minority interest and items could be purchased at modest cost. When he died at the age of eighty-one in 1856 the *Bristol Times* was to describe him as 'perhaps the largest collector of general and local antiquities in the West of England'. Most of the non-local collection was sold in the early twentieth century when the last of his children, William Jerdone Braikenridge (1817-1907), died. Although Braikenridge had six children who reached adulthood, only Jerdone (as he was known) married and there were no grandchildren. Another branch of the family, the Hales, were the heirs. The local collection was bequeathed to Bristol and a smaller, parallel collection illustrating Somerset, to Taunton.

The most important objects were sold in London in 1908 and some are now in museums. The finest piece, a magnificent twelfth-century enamel ciborium known to the Braikenridge family as 'The Malmesbury Ciborium', is now in New York in the Pierpont Morgan Library. A Gothic oak cradle which Braikenridge acquired purely for its romantic associations, as it was thought to be the cradle of Henry V, entered the Royal Collection and is usually on display in the Museum of London. It is now dated to the late fifteenth or early sixteenth century and is probably the only Gothic cradle in existence; Braikenridge had acquired it from another Bristol collection for 'above £30'. In 1834 he paid twelve guineas to a London dealer for a pair of thirteenth-century French copper-gilt and champlevé enamel candlesticks, which are now in the Metropolitan Museum of Art in New York. A fine silver parcel-gilt Elizabethan tazza (shallow cup) made in London in 1571 spent much of the twentieth century in private collections in America. It is now back in this country in an important private collection and is known as 'The Braikenridge Tazza'. The current location of many other ex-Braikenridge objects remains to be discovered but the most important is a 1534 mazer bowl (maple-wood drinking cup) with an inscription referring to the Tuckers, who perfected cloth in the medieval wool trade. It may once have been the property of the Tuckers' Guild whose hall was in Temple Street, Bristol.

The Braikenridges were of Scottish descent and first settled in Brislington, then a Somerset village, in the 1730s. George Weare Braikenridge's father, George Braikenridge (1738-1827), became a tobacco planter and merchant living in Hanover County, Virginia. He married there in 1772 and George Weare, his eldest son, was born in 1775. It was the year that the War of American Independence broke out. When he was about ten, the boy was sent to Bristol to be educated and he may have been brought up by his grandmother at Winash House, Brislington. His father finalised his American business and probably returned to Bristol in 1793 with his other two sons. Braikenridge's mother and two sisters certainly returned that year, but their ship the *Harriot* struck the Scarweather Sands in the Bristol Channel and had to be abandoned. Within six weeks all three had died of scarlet fever, a tragedy which was blamed on the shipwreck. Braikenridge was by now a young man, and he would barely have remembered his sisters as babies and had presumably never met his younger brothers before.

2 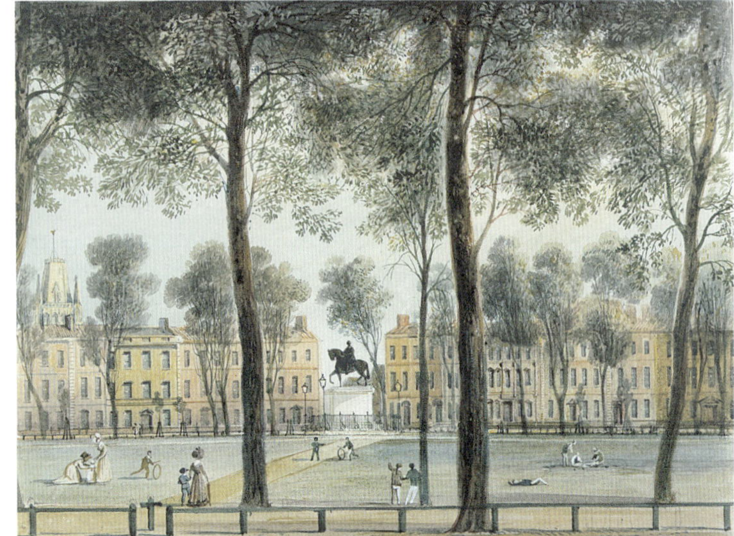

Queen Square, looking south-east 1827
Thomas L Rowbotham
Braikenridge lived at 21 Queen Square from 1809 to 1816. His home was the four-bayed stone-faced house in this drawing, near the tower of St Mary Redcliffe and immediately above the brown-suited boy with a hoop. Queen Square had been completed in the 1720s and was named after Queen Anne, who had died in 1714. There are only a few drawings of Georgian developments in the Braikenridge Collection as his main interest was in the older buildings.

Braikenridge joined his father's Dry-Salter's business in Temple Street and by 1797 it was known as George Braikenridge and Son. Dry-salters dealt in the chemical products used in drugs, preservatives, colour dyes, household cleaning materials and so on. After his father retired in 1802, Braikenridge progressed from dry-saltery into a partnership as a merchant with Richard Honnywill based in Queen Square. Braikenridge had married Mary Bush in 1800 and they first lived in Redcliffe Parade, moving to the Queen Square house in 1809 when the business transferred to The Back. Ten children were born between 1804 and 1817, and in 1816 or 1817 the family moved again, to Brislington.

Bristol's lucrative trade with the West Indies enabled Braikenridge to retire from business in 1820 when he was in his mid-forties. Away from commerce, his first enthusiasms had been for the natural sciences and he had notable collections of *Coleoptera* (beetles) and fossils but he had also begun his study of local history. An interest in British antiquity and county history had long been a pursuit of the gentry but in Braikenridge's youth it became much more common and was accentuated by the closure of Europe to tourist travel during the Revolutionary and Napoleonic wars. His long retirement was spent in quiet domestic harmony at Brislington and devoted to collecting and antiquarian studies. According to his obituary in the *Gentleman's Magazine* he was 'valued and loved' by those he knew well for his 'sterling qualities of character, kindness of disposition and demeanour, and great powers of conversation. He possessed a remarkable fund of local anecdote'.

Braikenridge purchased Broomwell House, a mid-eighteenth century house in Wick Road, Brislington, in May 1823. He spent the rest of his life there and created a setting for his antiquarian studies with a Gothic library as its centrepiece. This library, or 'museum' as it was also called, was an early example of what art historians now describe as an 'antiquarian interior', that is furnished with 'antiques' and modern fittings in an antique style. At Broomwell House in the 1820s, Gothic fitments were installed and the walls were decorated with carvings and paintings of Bristol interest. Genuine seventeenth-century furniture and a magnificent chimney-piece, rescued after fire destroyed a house in Small Street, were combined with furniture made-up of old carvings ('hybrid furniture') and contemporary furniture in the Gothic fashion. Some of the room, including an elaborate carved door, survives at a house in Clevedon to which Braikenridge's eldest son moved the room and its contents in the 1860s.

Braikenridge's principal memorial is his collection of topographical drawings of Bristol. He was not an artist himself, as is sometimes thought, but a collector who commissioned mainly local artists to record the city for him. The quality varies from amateur work to superb drawings by Bristol School artists, for Braikenridge was fortunate to be collecting in the 1820s when there was a talented group of artists working in the city.

The origins of Braikenridge's collection of images of Bristol lies in the gentlemanly hobby of extra-illustrating or 'grangerizing' books such as county and town histories. Books were not lavishly illustrated as they are today and it was common to add prints or drawings to a published text. (The term 'grangerize' was named after the eighteenth-century author the Reverend James Granger whose *Biographical History of England* was a common text for extra-illustration. Braikenridge had a copy of it, of course, and grangerized it with nearly 4000 portraits.) The chosen text was bought unbound, interleaved with additional illustrations, and then bound to match the other volumes in the gentleman's library. Print-dealers catered for this craze for extra-illustrating by stocking suitable prints. Some collectors, like Braikenridge, could afford to commission artists to draw subjects for them while others settled for amateur work. Many public libraries now care for these handsome volumes which have in themselves often become an important source for historians.

By the beginning of the nineteenth century about half of the English counties were covered by reasonably good histories. The inspiration for Braikenridge was William Barrett (c1727-1789) and his prodigious work, the *History and Antiquities of the City of Bristol*, published in 1789. Barrett's profession had been as a surgeon and man-midwife but his hobby was local history and he was Bristol's first historian. Braikenridge's 1400 drawings were

3

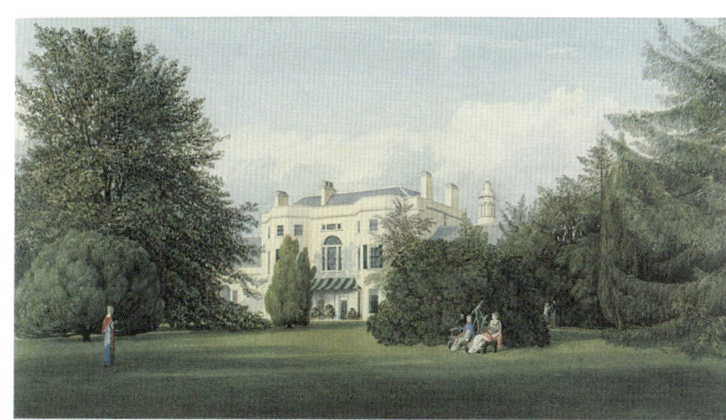

***Broomwell House, Brislington* c. 1823**
Samuel Jackson

Jackson made this watercolour soon after Braikenridge purchased Broomwell House. It shows the garden front, which looked out over fields towards Bristol. The other side of the house faced directly onto Wick Road, with no garden, and was very plain. The wing on the left, almost obscured by the large tree, has its original Venetian window. Braikenridge soon replaced it with one in the Gothic taste and used the room as his library.

Broomwell House was demolished in 1915.

not in the end bound with the text of Barrett's book but remained in folio albums. They do not stand alone, for as he acquired each drawing he catalogued it. Each was numbered on the back using an alpha-numeric system and the number, artist, date and subject were entered in a notebook. This was sound curatorial practice. In addition, the catalogue notes are an informative and delightful mix of diligent description and recording, observations on contemporary Bristol and snippets of gossip.

There was also a large complementary collection to the drawings, now in the Bristol Central Reference Library. It is the unbound text of Barrett's book interleaved with extra material carefully inlaid on same-size paper with a wash-line border. The bulk of this information was collected over a period of more than thirty years and originally filled thirty-six portfolios. However, the first known item he acquired was in 1803 and he was still making additions in the 1850s. His intention was to correct Barrett's errors, add new information and bring the history up-to-date with contemporary material such as the building of the Suspension Bridge, the arrival of the railway and the building of Brunel's great iron ships. There are newspaper cuttings, extracts from other books and periodicals, pamphlets, maps, engravings, business ephemera such as bill-heads, correspondence with other antiquaries, original documents and autograph letters, manuscript notes, and oddities such as a sample of fabric from the bed where Richard Cromwell slept in Lewin's Mead in 1657. Braikenridge's all-embracing and meticulous collecting was an end in itself for he had no intention of writing a definitive history of the city himself and simply called this part of the Bristol collection 'this collection of Scraps'.

The thirty-six portfolios and the 1400 drawings in the topographical collection were the organised part of his Bristol material. Both were arranged according to the chapters of Barrett's *History and Antiquities of the City of Bristol,* whose framework was the city's parishes. Braikenridge made additional sections such as the river courses. The two collections were obviously very closely related and contain numerous cross-references to each other.

However, these organised collections were only a part of Braikenridge's Bristol material. There were also albums of trade cards and bookplates, theatre programmes, brown paper packages of manuscript notes and a large library. When the library was catalogued in 1894 by the direction of Jerdone Braikenridge, a large section was devoted to Bristol material. There were volumes of Acts of Parliament relating to Bristol, albums of letters with Bristol connections, sale catalogues, sixteen folio volumes of collections of manuscripts (including the eighteenth-century Southwell Papers and the earlier Henley and Merchant Adventurers' Papers), notes on wills, and ephemera such as the rules of the Bristol Savings Bank and circulars concerning various Bristol charities. There were dozens of published works on Thomas Chatterton and a large number of Civil War pamphlets, booklets and broadsides. There were of course poll books, guidebooks and trade directories, along with parliamentary and municipal election material including the squibs (lampoons). Braikenridge also had a large number of newspapers including an eighteenth-century collection bound in folio volumes, import and export lists, and a mass of material classified under 'Trials and Crimes' which consisted largely of gruesome eighteenth-century pamphlets. All of this was in addition to the obvious topographical, historical and antiquarian publications on Bristol. An appendix catalogued books, including chap-books (pamphlets of popular tales and ballads), which indirectly related to the subject in that they were published or written in Bristol, or were published elsewhere by Bristolian authors, or were sermons that had been preached in Bristol. Friends helped him out with obscure titles; Richard Smith, a surgeon at the Infirmary with antiquarian interests, presented Braikenridge with the 1712 *Poetical Description of Bristol* and wondered if he already had it 'amongst your Stores in the Bristol Muniment Rooms'.

They were indeed muniment rooms, for Braikenridge also had a collection of 343 deeds, nearly 300 of which related to Bristol. Most dated from the fifteenth century. They included those which the poet Chatterton had cut off blank pieces to write his forgeries of medieval verse upon. Deeds were not hard to come by and were valued by few apart from antiquaries. They were often used by tailors for cutting out patterns or boiled-up by glue-makers. It was Jerdone Braikenridge who realised the importance of his father's deeds to students of local history and had a catalogue of them written by Francis B Bickley of the British Museum, published in 1899.

There were also many more prints, drawings, watercolours and oil paintings. Two more folio albums, called 'Views in Bristol and its Vicinity', probably included the other fifty Samuel Jackson (1794-1869) watercolours he owned; a splendid collection which were not part of the extra-illustrations to Barrett. There were also about a dozen oils and watercolours of local scenes by Francis Danby (1793-1861) and drawings by the eighteenth-century antiquarian draughtsman Samuel Hieronymus Grimm (1733-1794). Braikenridge also commissioned over 100 drawings, most by Thomas L Rowbotham (1782-1853), of the village of Brislington and its surroundings which are a remarkable record of the former appearance of one of Bristol's suburbs. Although Braikenridge was not a connoisseur of oil paintings he acquired some of largely local interest, many of which were portraits of Bristolians, from bishops to businessmen.

He also collected what he called Bristol 'relics'. They ranged from fragments of architecture to curiosities such as an old bottle or a ring found in the Floating Harbour. Corbels and barge-boards were rescued from buildings which were being demolished and incorporated into the gate-lodge at Broomwell House and elsewhere in his grounds. However, these relics were not saved forever and were lost when those buildings were demolished in their turn for the spread of suburbia. One Bristol relic that was saved for posterity is the pair of quarter boys on the façade of Christ Church, Broad Street. The boys had struck the hours on the original church which had been demolished in the eighteenth century and, after being cared for by several antiquaries and starring in the 1821 ceremony in Bristol for the Coronation of George IV, were bought by Braikenridge in 1824. They were returned to the City after the death of his sons and are now lent back to the church.

In 1837 Braikenridge wrote modestly of this overwhelming amount of material: 'For many years past I have diligently collected every antiquity and

4

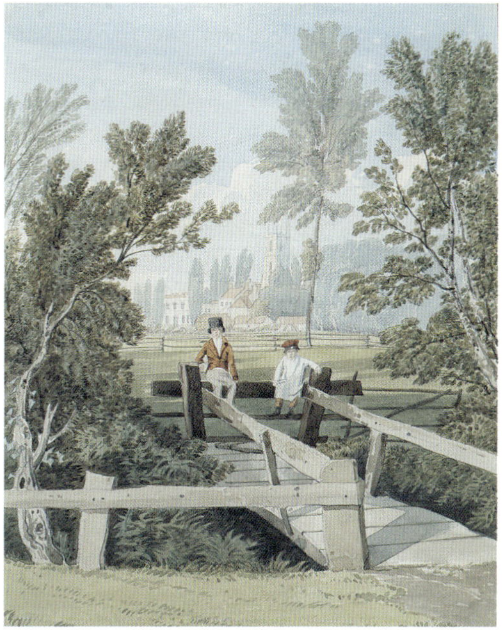

Two boys on a stile at Brislington Brook
c. 1824 Samuel Jackson

This charming scene is in Holy Meads field, now in the Kenneth Road area, looking towards the centre of Brislington village. The children may well have been Braikenridge's two sons; in 1824 George Weare junior would have been nine years old and his younger brother, William Jerdone, seven. Both boys were sent to Oxford and the elder then went into the Church, becoming the vicar of Christ Church, Clevedon.

M.S.S. [manuscripts] of all descriptions which could in any way relate to the History of Bristol'. Richard Smith was more fulsome about the achievements of 'the Brislington Collector of the Antiquities of Bristol – antiquities forsooth! not those only, but modern-ities also, in fact, all and every thing that relates to our city. Time, money, house-room – all have been unsparingly employed in the preservation of that which otherwise would have perished'. (*Bristol Mirror*, 21 October 1837).

Although Braikenridge wrote nothing himself except notes he was generous in providing access to his research material, as were his sons after his death, and he would have been gratified that his collections were used by Bristol's later historians. In 1881 the first volume of J.F. Nicholls and John Taylor's *Bristol Past and Present* was published with a dedication to the Reverend George Weare Braikenridge, who had made his father's collection available to the authors. In the 1890s John Latimer, who compiled the incomparable *Annals of Bristol*, knew of the drawings and had used some of the manuscript material. Jerdone Braikenridge had the perspicacity to bequeath all of this local material to Bristol if his heirs, the Hales, had no interest in it. It is now divided between the three specialist repositories of Bristol Record Office, Bristol Central Reference Library and Bristol Museums & Art Gallery. It is a measure of Braikenridge's thoroughness that his historical collections still serve as an essential source for local historians today and that the drawings are also consulted by family and social historians, archaeologists, planners and architects.

Although nearly forty artists are represented in the collection of drawings, over two-thirds of the work was done by three: Hugh O'Neill (441 drawings), Thomas L Rowbotham (258) and Joseph Manning (302). Hugh O'Neill (1784-1824) was an antiquarian draughtsman who spent the last four years of his life in Bristol. His work was predominantly monochrome wash over a precise pencil drawing and Braikenridge particularly admired his accuracy. Rowbotham and Joseph Manning (active1823-1832) succeeded him. Rowbotham lived in Bristol for about a decade from the mid-1820s and tackled all subjects and it is his lively street and dock scenes which add most character to the collection. Manning's work has not been included here as he was used mainly for ecclesiastical subjects of antiquarian interest and, although a diligent recorder, was not a distinguished artist. Other artists included in this selection are Samuel Jackson and James Johnson (1802/3-1834), who are both well-known artists of the Bristol School, and Edward Cashin (active 1822-26) and George William Delamotte (active 1822-1831) who are known only by their work for Bristol's antiquaries.

The organisation of the Bristol collection was a retirement project and most of the drawings were acquired in the 1820s, with a trickle of additions in the 1830s. When O'Neill arrived in Bristol from Bath in 1820, Braikenridge tells us he met him by 'chance'. It seems that this chance encounter provided the impetus for extra-illustrating Barrett. With the exception of a few drawings O'Neill made for Samuel Seyer's *Memoirs of Bristol*, published 1822-5, he was 'alone employed' by Braikenridge and at his untimely death in 1824 still had a list of over thirty subjects which his patron had wanted drawn. He must also have had an understanding with Braikenridge that he should draw anything he considered of interest. For example, in 1822 he joined forces with Henry Smith, another enthusiastic local antiquary (who by profession was an attorney) to clean a monumental figure in St Philip's Church which had been choked with numerous coats of limewash. O'Neill then drew it in its improved state. He also recorded the city in the act of change, from the demolition of an old house to the erection of a new gas works.

The acquisition of the collection seems to have been a random process and Braikenridge did not work on one area of the city at a time. It is remarkable that in such a large collection there are so few duplications. Like O'Neill, Rowbotham and Manning suggested subjects as well as working to commission, but the collection also grew in a variety of other ways. Several drawings were gifts, for example from fellow Bristol antiquary William Tyson or the Reverend John Eden, vicar of St Nicholas' and a friend of many years. Eden was an amateur sketcher in sepia, and although a kindly man had little artistic talent. There are many of his drawings in the collection and they sit uncomfortably with the overall quality of most of the work. Another amateur was Miss Bird, daughter of the Bristol artist Edward Bird RA (1772-1819). She made naïve and romantic watercolours of imaginary scenes which were intended as frontispieces to certain Barrett chapters. 'Matilda entering Bristol Castle' would have preceded the Castle chapter, and 'Funeral of Canynges' that of St Mary Redcliffe. Braikenridge also bought drawings from local booksellers who stocked prints and drawings. There was little need for him to purchase the work of national artists when such competent local artists were available, but he did buy a few drawings by well-known topographical artists such as William Henry Bartlett (1809-1854) and John Chessell Buckler (1793-1894).

Much of the charm of Braikenridge's catalogue of his drawings lies in the entries that reveal something of the man himself. Along with the topographical descriptions and antiquarian information there are personal prejudices and idiosyncracies. He can be prim, as when reporting that Dr Beake the Dean of Bristol Cathedral 'with a great deal of good feeling' had nailed down the most indecent misericords to prevent them being improperly exposed. We not only learn about the functions of buildings but sometimes of the people who lived in them. When Rowbotham drew Pile Street Braikenridge wrote 'The whole of this Street is inhabited by Persons of the lowest description'. When the same artist drew King Street he was more interested in customs than architecture: 'The Llandoger Trow has long been a celebrated public House and frequented by many Persons in the Evenings for the express purpose of drinking Ale' (which of course it still is). There are also a few glimpses of him collecting information. There was a Mr Isaac James, a 'Deacon of the Baptist Persuasion' 'who is not only possessed of much information on old Bristol History but willing to communicate it when required' and a Mr Terrel who gave him a long account of how a mason had carried out the daring feat of removing the weathercock from the spire of St Nicholas' to repair its tail after a soldier had wantonly fired his musket at it. Although he regretted much of the destruction of older buildings he could also be appreciative of good contemporary work; in 1831 he wrote of the building which is now the Arnolfini gallery that Messrs Acramans had cleared the site and 'erected a most superb warehouse'.

Braikenridge had collected the majority of his Bristol drawings by the end of the 1820s and in the 1840s he embarked upon a similar project by grangerizing a copy of John Collinson's *History and Antiquities of the County of Somerset*, published in 1791. It is now in the collection of the Somerset Archaeological and Natural History Society in Taunton. The drawings and other material were originally interleaved and bound up with Collinson's text in folio volumes but most are unfortunately now dismembered. The collection is disappointing in comparison with the Bristol drawings as the quality of the work is not so high and, as Braikenridge was not so familiar with his subject, it lacks his personal touch. Although there are a few drawings by Bristol School artists the main contributor was William Walter Wheatley (*c*1811-1885) who spent ten years travelling throughout the county for his patron. Although he was an indifferent draughtsman, he was a good choice in that he was a diligent antiquary himself in searching out information and subject matter.

Antiquaries are often represented as being without discrimination and there are many eighteenth-century caricatures of them engrossed in the minutiae of history. Walter Scott wrote *The Antiquary* (1815) and gently poked fun at their obsessions; gently, for he was an antiquary himself. Without the antiquaries much would have been lost, for they were the early archaeologists and social, local and architectural historians who strove to record the past in the days before conservation societies. Objects of curiosity in their collections, such as the Gothic cradle which was thought to have been Henry V's, only survived because a succession of antiquaries cared for it for its romantic associations with royalty.

Braikenridge's recording of his own times, as well as the past, in his comprehensive collection of topographical drawings and manuscript material has been vindicated by their survival in Bristol's and Taunton's public collections. Bristol is well-recorded by early photography but the Braikenridge Collection of drawings allows us to step back another generation to the 1820s and to the end of the Georgian era. The city before Braikenridge is known through maps, plans and a limited number of images. His achievement allows us to visualize the historic city above the ground and brings to life the lines on the map. The drawings received national recognition in 1998 when Bristol Museums & Art Gallery was 'Designated' by the Museums & Galleries Commission and its Braikenridge Collection, from which this book has been selected, was recognised as a collection of exceptional quality.

5 ***The church of St John-on-the-Wall, looking towards the Quay* 1828**

Thomas L Rowbotham

Bristol's port extended into the centre of the city and the bustle and activity of the quaysides provided much of the city's character. Its attractions were often commented upon by visitors. The Braikenridge Collection shows how the city's appearance was dominated by the water, both of the River Frome and the Floating Harbour. With its medieval street pattern, picturesque buildings and constant glimpses of water, how like Venice Bristol might have been!

St John the Baptist Church, commonly called St John-on-the-Wall, was built on the town wall and its tower stands over what was the northern gate of the medieval town. It was not until 1542 that Bristol was granted city status.

On the left, two young women are collecting water from the conduit in Nelson Street, which had recently been moved from its position under the tower (see following drawing). The water has come to St John's from a spring on Brandon Hill for over 600 years. It was first piped to a Carmelite Friary, on the site of the Colston Hall, in 1267. In 1376, the Friary gave permission for a branch pipe to supply the parishioners of St John's.

There is now a Victorian fountain outside the church which the City Council hopes to have flowing again soon. The pipeline from Brandon Hill, which had broken in several places in Trenchard Street, is being repaired at the time of writing. It will be one of the few British medieval conduits still in working order.

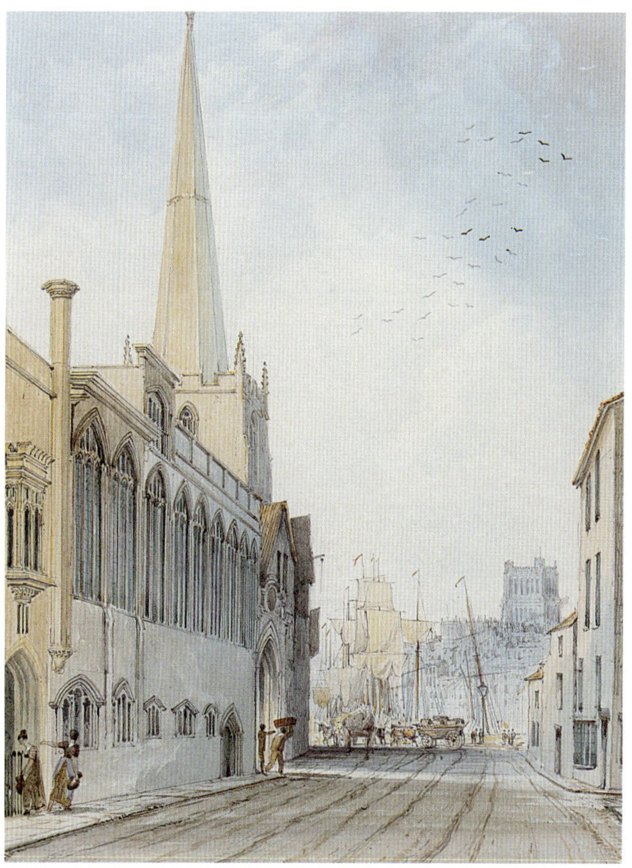

6 ***St John's Conduit and Tower Lane* 1825**

George W Delamotte

A boy and a dog can be seen at the water supply on the left. In 1827 this ornate seventeenth-century conduit house was demolished and the water diverted to a fountain (see previous drawing) set in the north wall of the same church, St John-on-the-Wall. Moving the conduit allowed room for another arch for pedestrians to be opened up through the wall. There had previously been several serious accidents to women and children waiting near the conduit under the narrow central arch, which connects Broad Street to Nelson Street.

Some houses, especially in Clifton, were fortunate enough to be connected to nearby springs. Others had wells, although these were often contaminated, but the poor were dependent on the public conduits and pumps. Bristol had woefully inadequate water supplies and an 1845 Royal Commission report on public health was to say 'there are few, if any, large towns in England in which the supply of water is so inadequate as at Bristol'. The Bristol Water Works Company was established in 1846 and began the formidable engineering work to bring water to the city from the Chew valley, some fifteen miles to the south. Houses paid a water rate to be connected, as they still do to the same company.

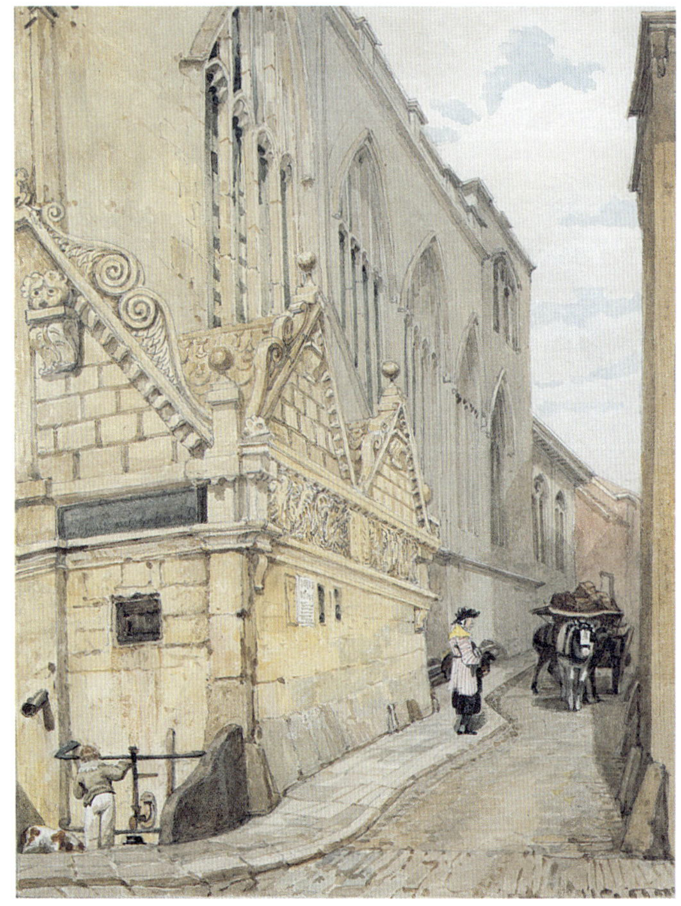

7 ***Broad Street* 1824**

Edward Cashin

We are looking up Broad Street towards Christ Church and, in the distance, the Dutch House. Just in front of the church, where the Grand Hotel now stands, are the White Hart and White Lion inns. The two boys in the right foreground are outside the door of the Guildhall and in front of a butcher's shop where a carcass hangs at an open window. Braikenridge remarked that there were few of these open-fronted shops left in Bristol by the 1820s. The butcher is trading from a handsome seventeenth-century timber-framed building.

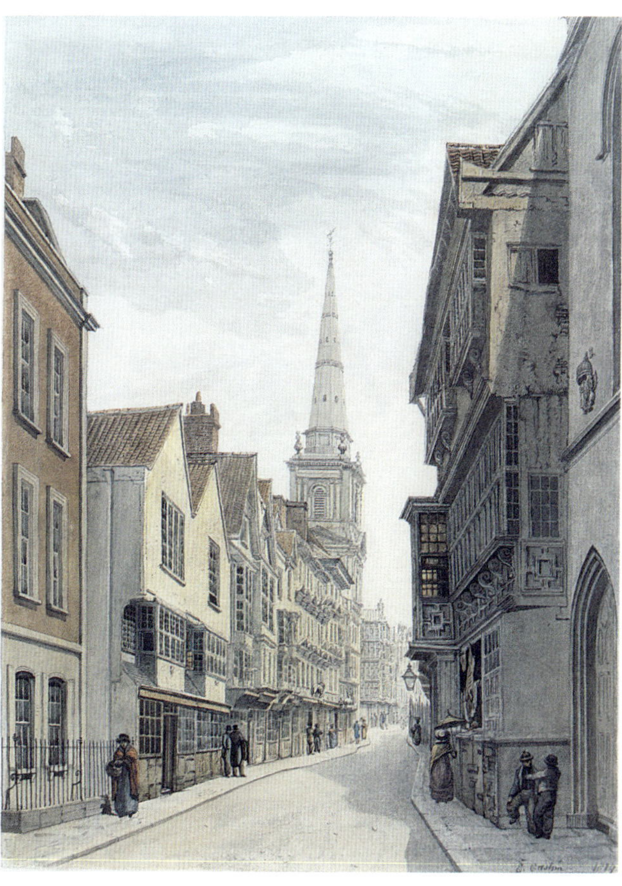

The appearance of the Dutch House is well-known from photographs so a drawing of it has not been reproduced here. It was said, incorrectly, that its façade had been brought to Bristol from Holland or Germany, and the name endures today with those who remember the building. It stood on the corner of High Street and Wine Street and was destroyed after being bombed in the Blitz. A corner post with a grotesque figure, dated 1676, is preserved in the Museum's collection.

8 ***St Leonard's Lane* 1823**

Hugh O'Neill

This lane, which still exists, originally followed the inside line of the medieval town walls and led from the northern end of Small Street to St Leonard's Church in Corn Street. St Leonard's had been demolished in 1771 to ease traffic congestion. We are looking in the direction of Corn Street, so the remains of the walls were on the right-hand side of this drawing. Braikenridge records that a boys' and a girls' school had been built into the walls. Washing hangs on a line strung across the street and almost dangles in the central gutter.

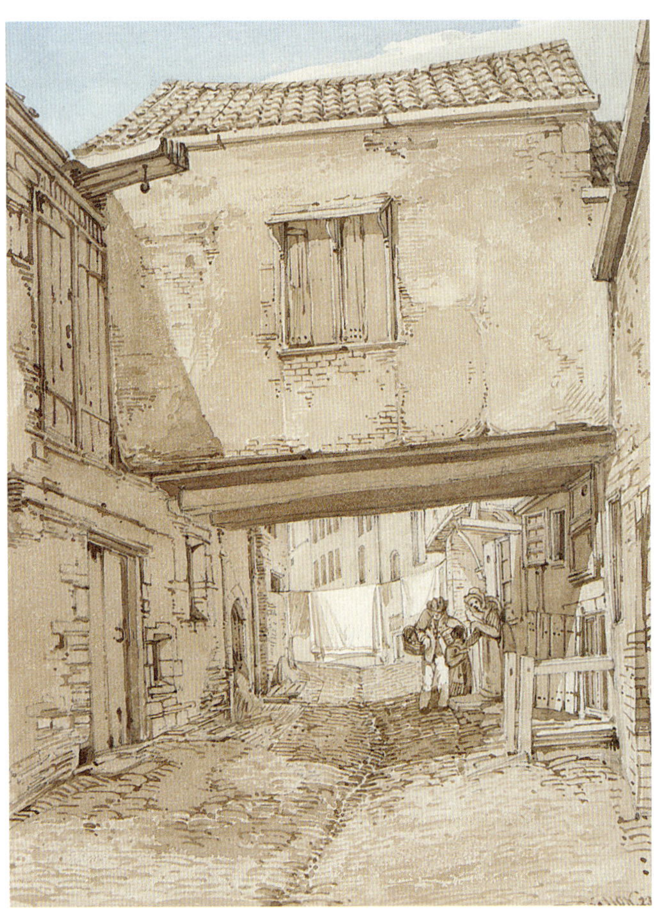

9 ***The Front of the Taylors' Hall, Taylors' Court, off Broad Street* 1823**

Hugh O'Neill

During the eighteenth century the Taylors (tailors) were one of the twenty-three surviving trade companies in the city but they ceased to exist on the death of their last member, Isaac Amos, in 1824. For as long as he lived he solemnly carried out the Guild's customs by electing himself Master, notifying himself of meetings and so on.

This façade of the Taylors' Hall with its fine shell hood and coat-of-arms over the entrance still exists, although the interior has been converted into offices. The Hall was built in 1740-1 to replace an earlier building. Broad Street is seen through the arch at the end of the court.

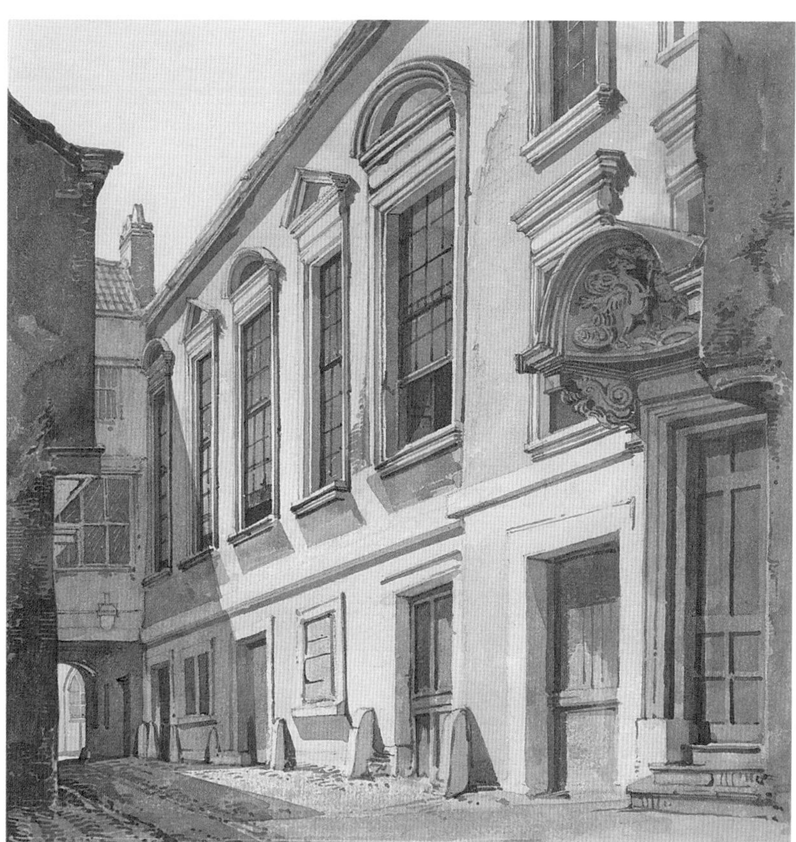

10 ***The (Old) Council House, Corn Street* 1822**

James Johnson

This drawing by the best architectural draughtsman in the Braikenridge Collection records the appearance of the early-eighteenth century Council House, soon to be demolished and replaced with a larger one. Braikenridge's notes record it had a hall at street level where the mayor and aldermen attended to administer public justice on days called Sword Days. Before the reform of local government in the 1830s the self-elected Corporation (Council) performed the function of magistrates. The Council Chamber was on the first floor.

The adjacent buildings are in Corn Street, with the famous Bush Inn towards the end of the row.

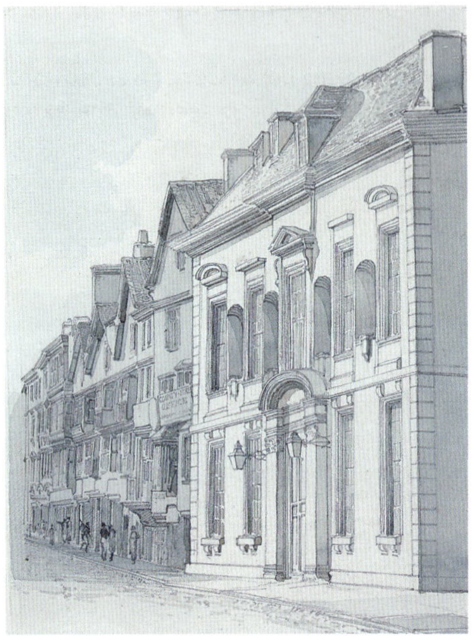

11 ***Looking down Broad Street with the New Council House* 1825**

Thomas L Rowbotham

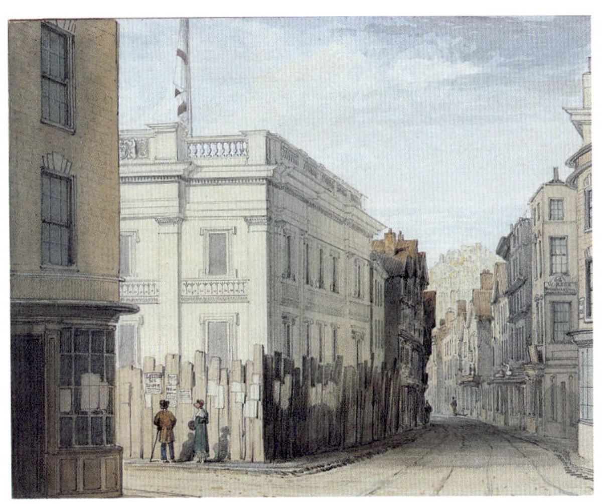

The former Council House (see previous drawing) had been demolished and a new one, designed by Sir Robert Smirke, was erected on the same site. The palings are not yet removed from this new Council House and one of the posters pasted on them gives details of the lottery. Braikenridge noted that the drawing was made on September 15th and a flag was flying on the building as that was the day the new mayor was chosen. The building was not completed and occupied for about another eighteen months. This building is now referred to as the Old Council House as the offices moved to an impressive new building on College Green, opened in 1956.

St Michael's Hill is in the distance and Braikenridge wrote of it in his catalogue: 'The Houses beyond the end of the Street, towering one above the other have a fine effect'.

12 ***The Laying of the Foundation Stone of the New Council House* 1824**

Edward Cashin

We are looking down Corn Street towards today's City Centre, with All Saints' on the left. The mayor laid the foundation stone in May 1824 and he is seen on the extreme right with the City Sword Bearer (in red) behind him. There had been a grand procession which had marched the long way around from the Guildhall in Broad Street via the Quay, St Stephen's Street and Corn Street. It included members of the Council, the Merchants' Society, the Incorporation of the Poor, clergy, citizens and schoolchildren. Evidently a large crowd had assembled to watch the spectacle.

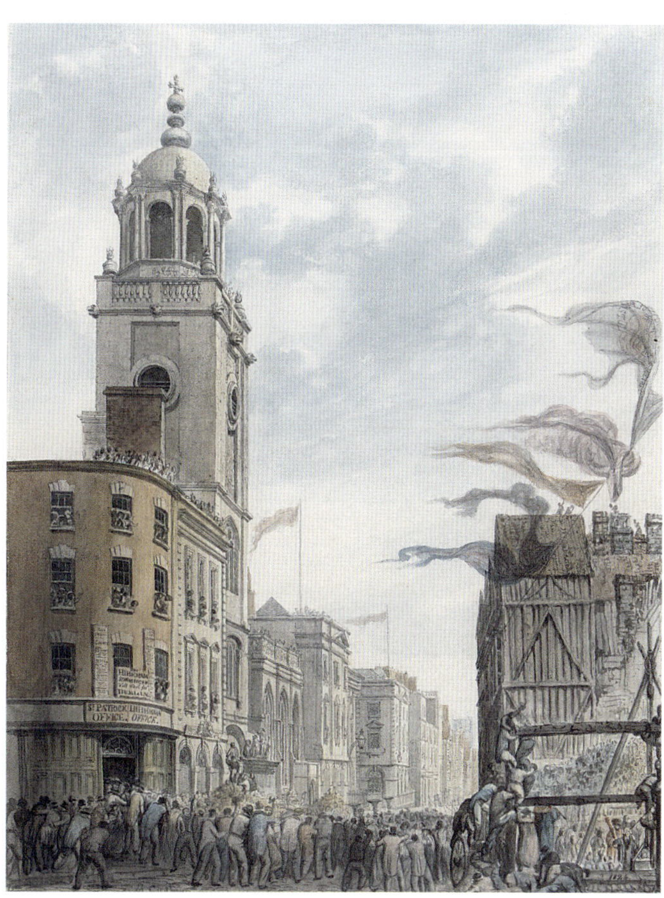

13 ***Cider House Passage* 1820**

Hugh O'Neill

Cider House Passage was an alley which ran east from Broad Street to join Tower Lane and this drawing is of the Broad Street end. The drawing opposite shows the medieval hall which was in the building over the alley. The building which catches the light was a sixteenth-century house constructed against it. The tall, one-bay extension on the right, next to a Gothic window, was probably a privy block.

In 1821 the rough ground in the foreground was built upon, for in the middle of Bristol every piece of land needed to be utilised.

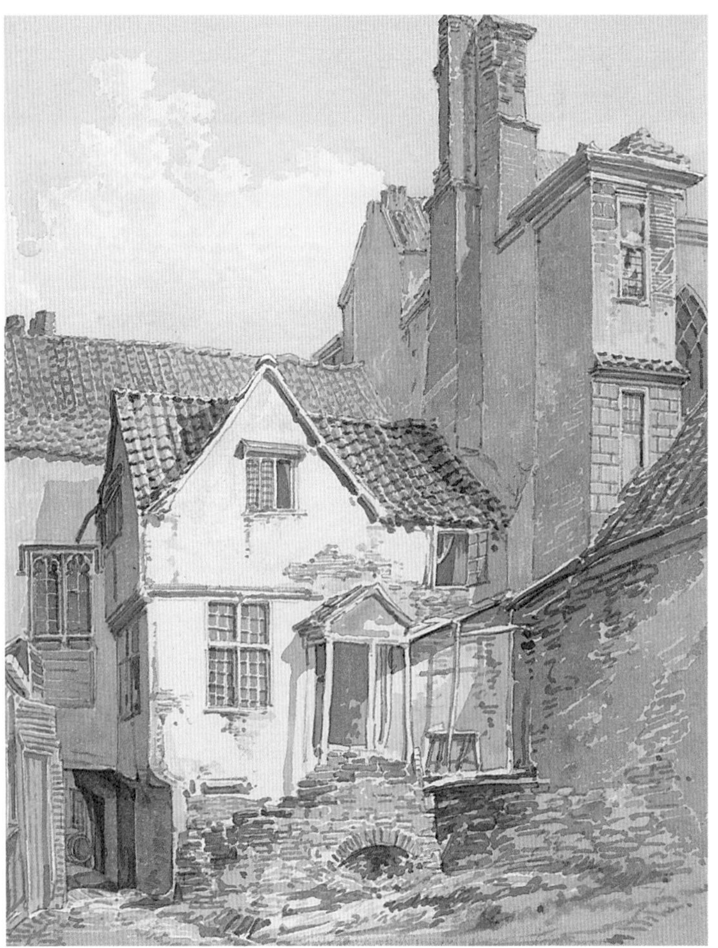

14 ***Room in a house in Cider House Passage* 1828**

Thomas L Rowbotham

The drawing opposite, of Cider House Passage, shows this room's Gothic window above the alley. This was a medieval hall, built on the first floor, with an arch-braced collar roof, and the two-light window was probably fourteenth-century. There had been much sub-division of the hall to adapt it for later use. Braikenridge, who was writing in the years before the history and sequence of English architectural styles had been defined, simply called it 'an ancient Room'.

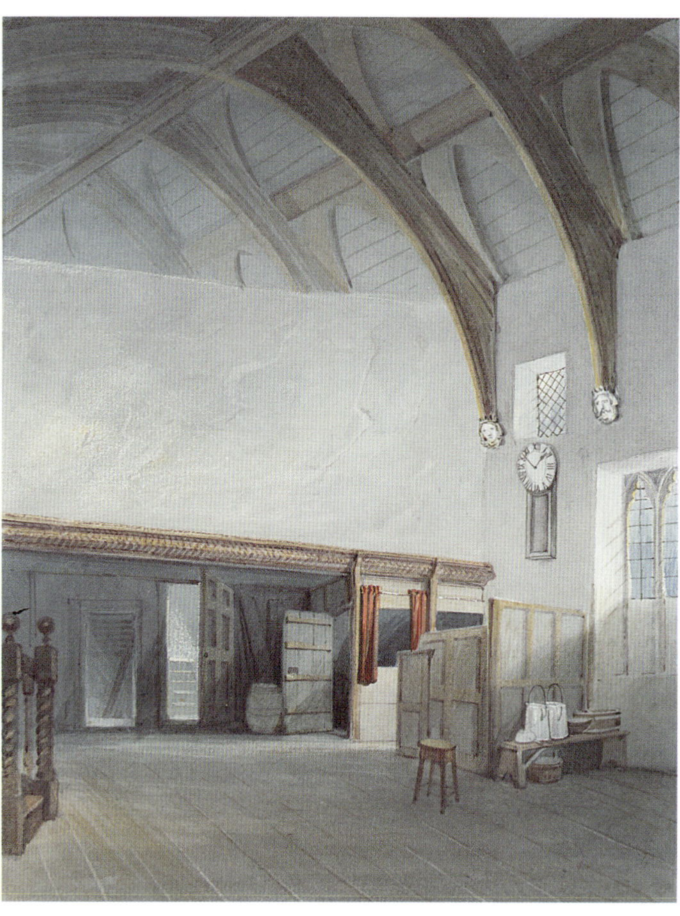

The room was later used for concerts but was then accidentally destroyed. In 1859 a fire broke out in the tavern in Cider House Passage, spread to the hall and destroyed much of it. When the site was excavated in 1990 the original building was found to be a Norman house, with many later additions. An end wall of it remains built into the Court House in Taylors' Court.

15 ***Corn Street* 1828**

Thomas L Rowbotham

We are standing at the junction of Corn Street and St Stephen's Street looking towards the towers of St Werburgh's Church (on the left) and All Saints', with the Dutch House in the distance. The Corn Exchange cannot be seen as it is set back from the street, nearly opposite St Werburgh's. The street was only about six metres wide by this tower and was one of the busiest in Bristol. The church was taken down in 1878 and much of it, including the tower, was re-erected at the new St Werburgh's in Mina Road.

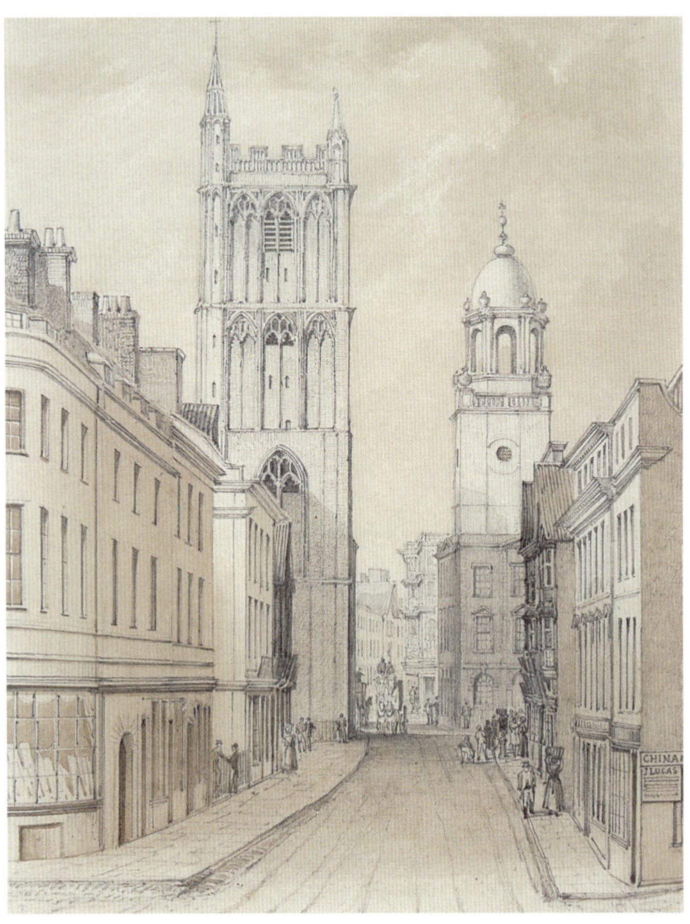

16 ***Looking up Small Street towards the Exchange* 1828**

Thomas L Rowbotham

The signboard on the left was for Smith, Son & Co. wholesale linen merchants and Manchester goods (cottons) at 24 Small Street. The street architecture has a marvellous mixture of styles. There is a Gothic arch on the left, and two doors further up a building converted into Smith's warehouse. This is followed by a jettied house of the sixteenth-century or earlier, the pink render of a Georgian façade and, in Corn Street, John Wood's Palladian Corn Exchange of 1741-3. St Werburgh's is on the right and the spire of St Nicholas' is in the distance.

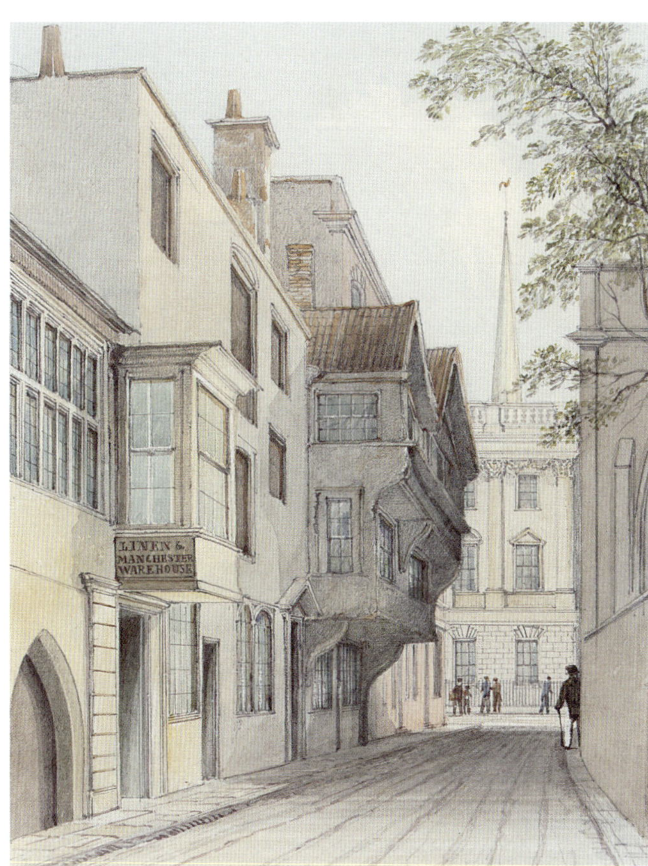

17 ***The supposed 'Crypt of St Leonard's Church'* 1827**
Thomas L Rowbotham

St Leonard's Church had been one of the medieval churches which stood on the old town wall. It had obstructed the end of Corn Street and was demolished in 1771 to allow the construction of Clare Street and give access to the Quay. As early as the 1820s, the two chambers underneath 16 Corn Street, on the corner of St Nicholas' Street, were erroneously presumed to have been its crypt.

The myth of the crypt continued until late in the twentieth century when archaeologists reviewed the evidence. It is now considered to have been simply a merchant's cellar, for it was not in the correct position for St Leonard's Church and also resembles other known cellars. One of the chambers is seen here; the floor level had been raised at some point, for the man is standing at the height of the springing of its arch.

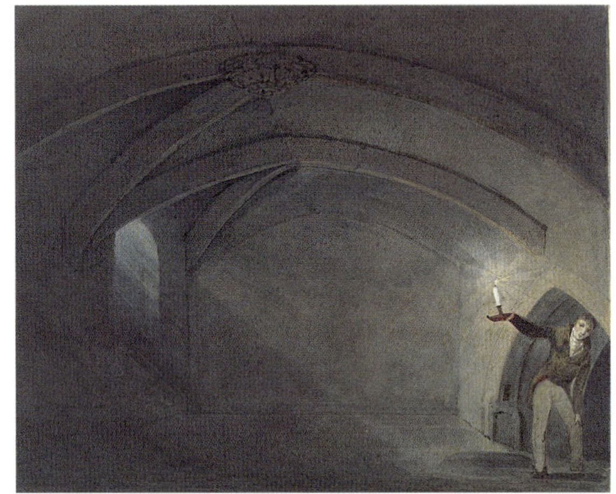

18 ***Crypt of St Lawrence's Church* 1827**
Thomas L Rowbotham

St Lawrence's Church had stood next to St John-on-the-Wall. It had closed in 1580 and was partially demolished soon after although the west end wall was there until the 1960s. Other drawings in the Braikenridge Collection show how arches and beams still remained in what were now commercial buildings. This crypt was underneath Nelson Street and was used as a mill for grinding barilla, an ash of burnt seaweed imported from Spain and the Levant. The lumps on the floor are the barilla, which was ground up to make soda.

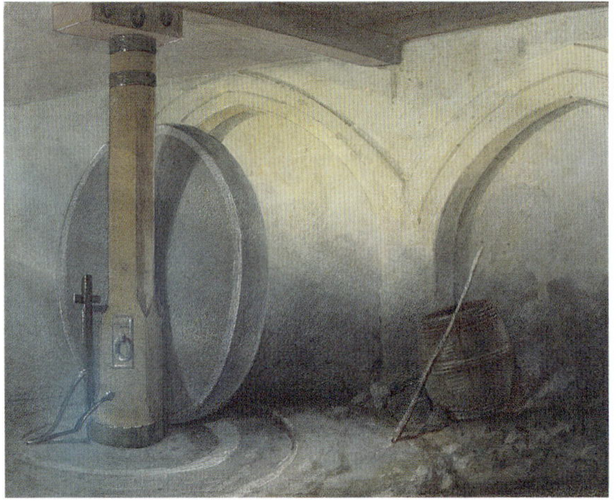

19 ***Guard House Passage, Wine Street* 1820**

James Johnson

The arch was built about 1520 with limestone from a quarry on Dundry Hill. It has seen many uses. It was first the entrance to a mansion, and then to a meal market (for flour etc.). It became the entry to a guard house for soldiers in the seventeenth century, then slipped into disrepair but was renovated for a garrison when a French invasion was feared during the Napoleonic Wars. After the reform of local government in the mid-1830s, the Council was obliged to set up a police force and for a few years the central station was at the Guard House. In 1881 the Guard House Arch was taken down and set up in a garden in Bishopston before becoming part of the Museum's collection where it is on permanent display.

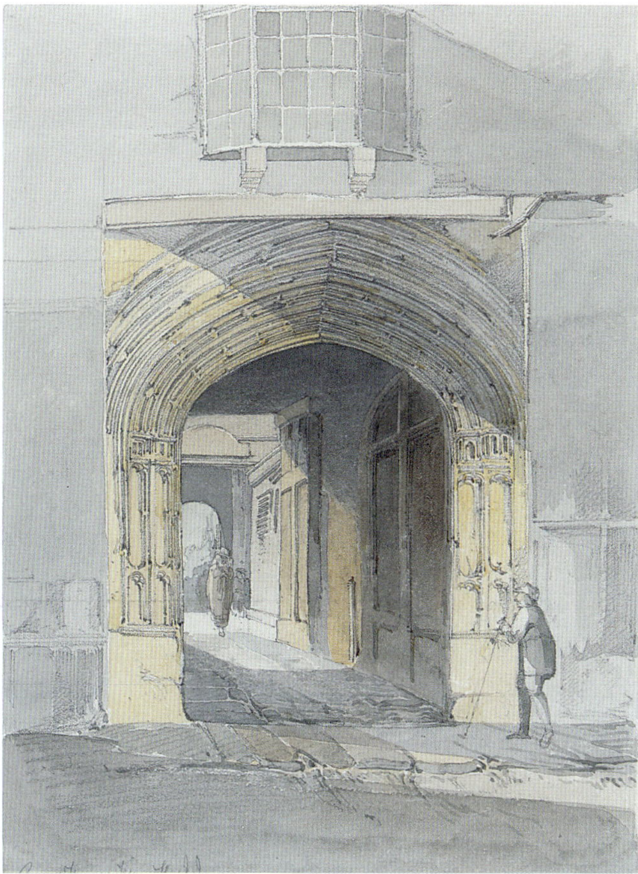

20 ***The discovery of an east window in All Saints' Church*** **1821**

James Johnson

On the night of 14 December, 1819, a fire broke out in High Street and destroyed four houses. It was not brought under control until it had spread as far as the corner facing the Council House and it was only just stopped from spreading to the opposite side of High Street and the Castle Bank (Dutch House). Nearly two years later this window was discovered when the damaged walls of the houses built up against All Saints' were removed. The window was walled up again when the houses were re-built.

Fire spread rapidly through the old timber-framed housing in the narrow streets of central Bristol and Braikenridge sometimes acquired fitments from buildings which had survived a fire. Robert Southey, the Bristol-born poet laureate, wrote in his *Letters from England*, 1807, that fire was 'a tremendous calamity which is everyday occurring in England' and that 'the traveller who is at London without seeing a fire, and at Naples without witnessing an eruption of Vesuvius, is out of luck.'

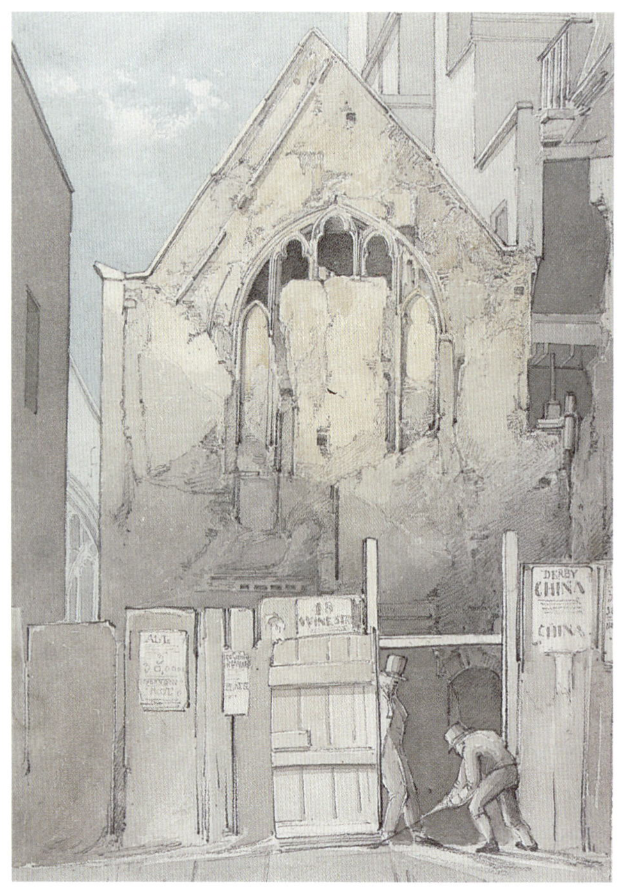

21 ***Wine Street 1826***

Thomas L Rowbotham

Wine Street was a fashionable shopping area; here we see a hatter, hosier and a woollen draper. Goss & Fowler were 'Manufacturers of Hosiery and Lace, Mercers, Haberdashers, and Glovers'. The passageway to the left of their shop (beneath the '7') led to the busy Plume of Feathers coaching inn. The spire of Christ Church is behind.

Despite being a fashionable street, it was also the site of public whippings. The Wine Street Pump, a public water supply, was near the entrance to the Pithay and was where those convicted of minor theft, or simply being a public nuisance, were flogged while a crowd watched.

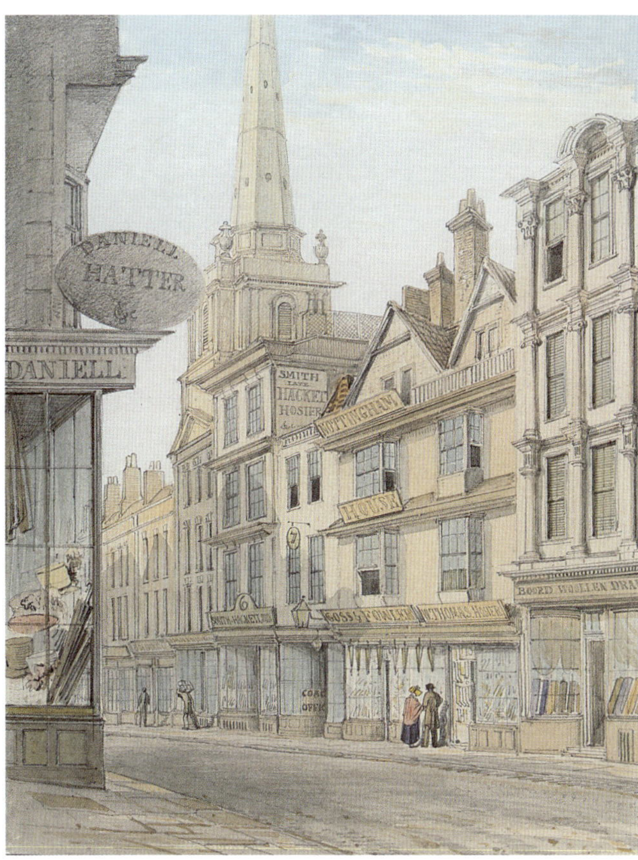

22 ***Top of the Pithay* 1829**

Thomas L Rowbotham

If you entered the Pithay from Wine Street this was the house which faced you. Many of the shops here dealt in second-hand clothes and furniture and it was also known as Broker's Alley. Braikenridge's notes recorded the house was 'formerly used to lock up Persons when first arrested for Debt & called the Spunging House'. A sponging- or spunging-house was a bailiff's lodging-house for debtors before they were committed to prison.

The Pithay itself descends steeply to the right to the Frome and the alley, under the sign for Charles Cummins the upholsterer and cabinet maker, is Tower Lane. The name Pithay originated from puit (well) and hai (stone enclosure). O'Neill made a drawing for Braikenridge showing the Pithay Pump, not included in this book, where people could draw water from the well.

The street was demolished in the late 1890s for the expansion of Fry's chocolate factories, which by then dominated this area. The seventeenth-century plaster coat-of-arms of the Guild of Brewers on the façade of this house was then presented to the Museum by the New Streets Committee.

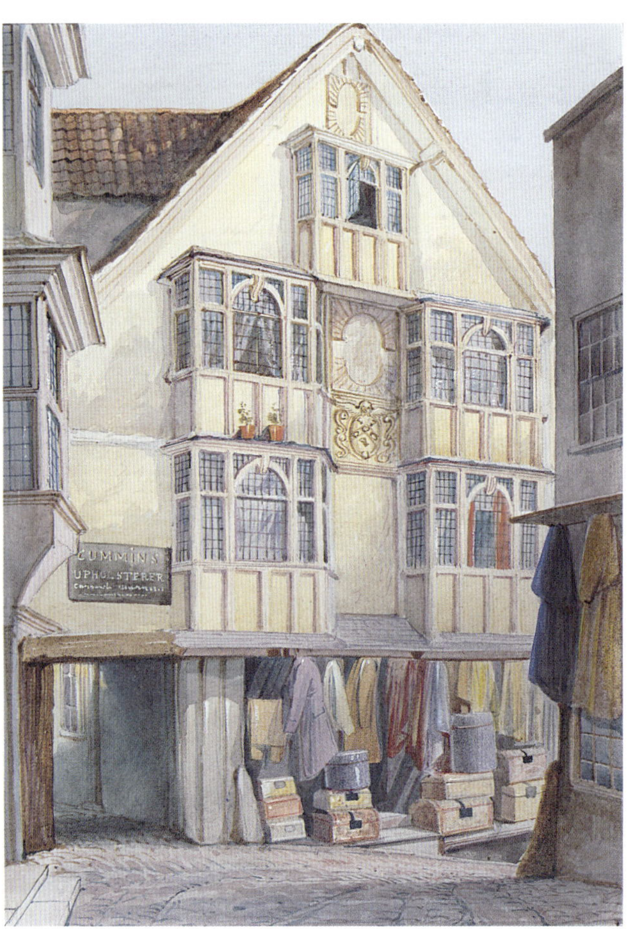

23 ***Tower Lane* 1820**

Hugh O'Neill

Tower Lane was an intra-mural lane following the inside of the first town wall from the church of St John-on-the-Wall (see plate 6) to the Pithay. A section of it remains today. Braikenridge's catalogue notes on this area included: 'Tower lane has long been the residence of profligate women & the small public Houses in and about that street are full [of] the dissolute of the other sex.'

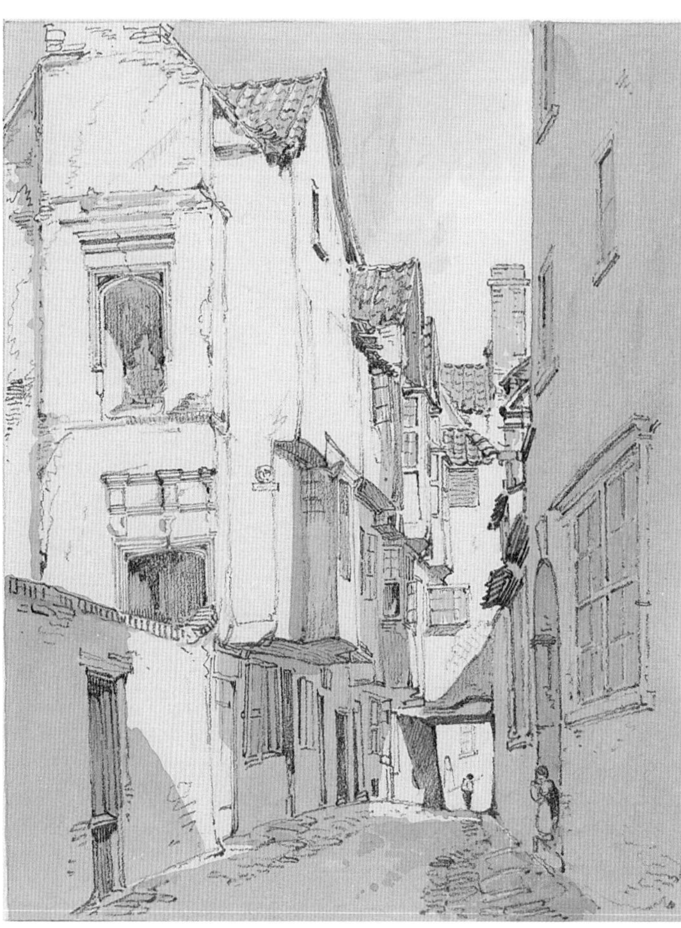

Internal features have been revealed by the demolition of a building on the left, with a door-frame above and a seventeenth-century chimney-piece below.

24 ***The bottom of High Street 1826***

Thomas L Rowbotham

The large windowless façade in shadow is the east end of St Nicholas' Church. Beyond, Welsh trading vessels are moored near Bristol Bridge.

The Angel Inn or Tavern had a very narrow façade on High Street of less than five metres. Its plan was 'L'-shaped and there was another frontage on St Nicholas' Street, which is the narrow opening just below the tobacconist's. In 1864 that corner building was demolished to widen St Nicholas' Street. This so weakened the Angel that in the following year it collapsed into the space left by its neighbour and Bristol lost another fascinating building.

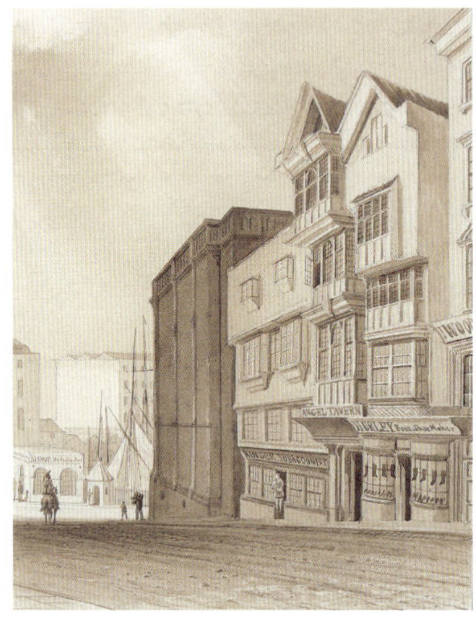

25 ***Chimney-piece at the Angel Inn, High Street 1820***

Hugh O'Neill

The chimney-piece appears to date from about 1350. It may have been adapted from stonework intended for a screen or similar, as the segmental arched opening has been cut out to enlarge the fireplace at some stage. The property which became the Angel Inn was rebuilt in the 1470s and re-fronted in the early seventeenth century.

The chimney-piece is now in the Museum's collection. The Museum purchased it in 1910 from the Fine Arts Academy (now the Royal West of England Academy) who had presumably cared for it for at least some of the years after the collapse of the building.

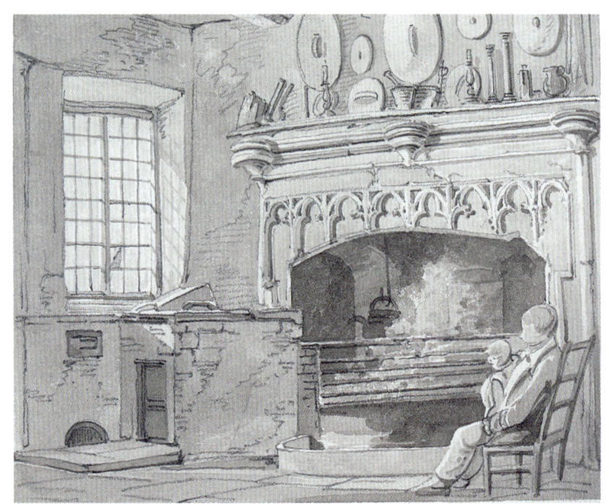

26 ***An upstairs room in the Angel Inn, High Street*** **1821**
Hugh O'Neill

The Angel Inn was a typical medieval property, narrow and deep. This drawing of the former hall is a good example of a converted medieval building which had been built on a tight urban site, with later sub-divisions of the hall. Large sixteenth or seventeenth-century windows have been fitted into the arch-braced collar roof of the side wall, which faced St Nicholas' Street. Braikenridge tells us the stairs on the left led to a billiard room.

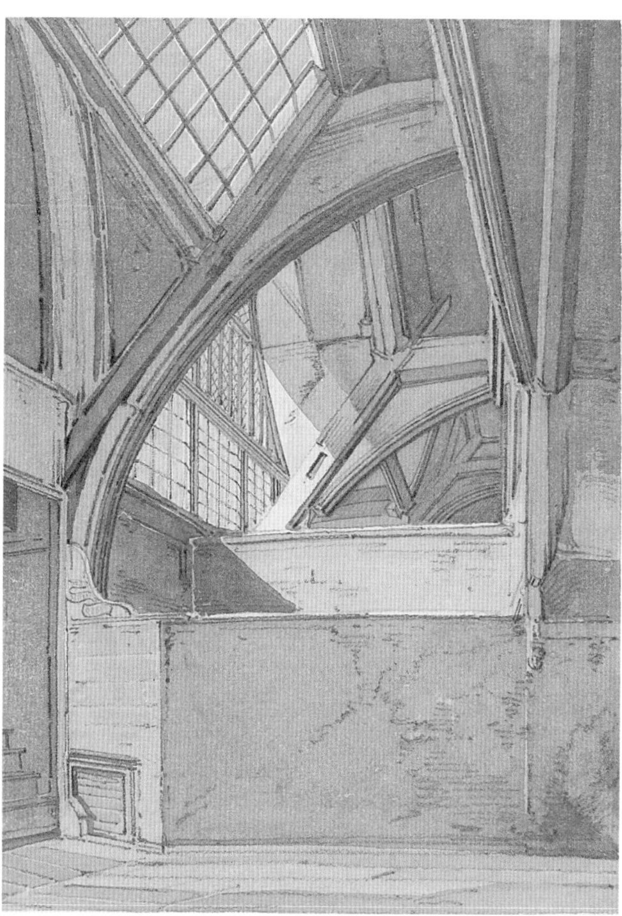

27 ***Mary-le-Port Street* 1824**

George W Delamotte

Mary-le-Port Street (or Mary Port Street) was narrow and dark where it joined High Street; here we can only just glimpse the market entrance beyond. This entrance still stands as the entrance to the market from High Street today.

By the 1820s, the timber-framed buildings which overhung many of the streets were regarded as very old-fashioned and inconvenient. Many were in poor repair and these have been braced for stability. They were frequently replaced or modernised with Georgian façades and shop fronts, as here. Despite the English weather, goods were often displayed outside shops. As well as the abundance of baskets, there are also shoes hung outside the shop on the right.

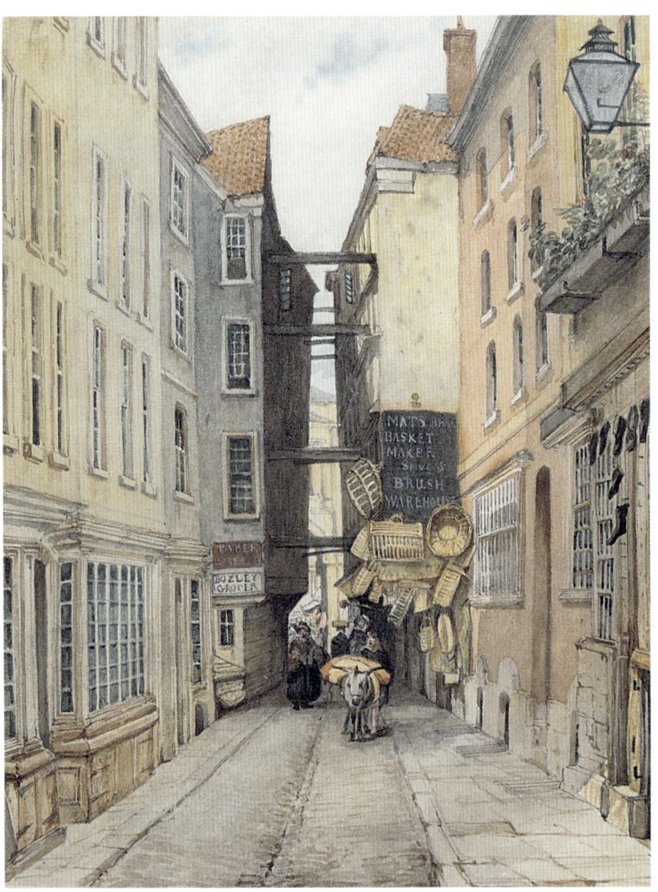

28 ***Peter Street and Mary-le-Port Street* 1826**

Thomas L Rowbotham

The gabled building on the left was built in 1613; its date is inscribed above the ground floor windows. It had once been the parsonage for St Peter's Church but by this time was occupied by a basket-maker. Twelve years after this drawing was made it was badly damaged by fire. Braikenridge recorded in a notebook that in September 1838 it was rebuilt and 'The Bargeboards & carved beams so often drawn are now in my possession & sent down to Clevedon to ornament the Gables of (my) coach house (at) Claremont Villa'. This was the Braikenridges' summer residence. The coach house is now living accommodation and the bargeboards have long-since disappeared, doubtless worn away by the weather.

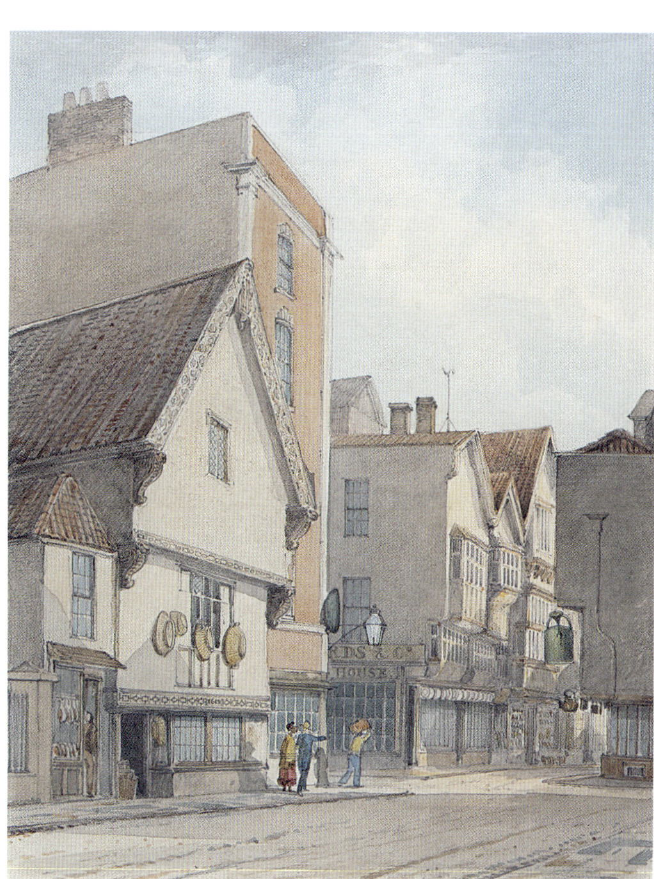

The giant watering-can advertises the premises of J & W Parnell, ironmongers in Mary-le-Port Street. Opposite, on the corner of Dolphin Street, hats hang in a row outside William Edwards & Co., hatter and hosier.

29 ***Interior of St Peter's Church* 1828**

James Johnson

In the summer of 1828 Johnson made over a dozen fine drawings of church interiors. They are a valuable record of the churches' appearance before they were substantially changed during the Victorian Gothic Revival.

These box pews in St Peter's had replaced medieval ones in 1698 and at the east end is a Baroque reredos. Several of these reredos were installed in Bristol at the beginning of the eighteenth century but the only one which survives today is in St Thomas'. With the liturgical emphasis on preaching, St Peter's pulpit has a sounding board to help carry the voice.

The church was bombed in 1940 and its shell remains in memory of the citizens of Bristol and the surrounding areas who died during the Blitz.

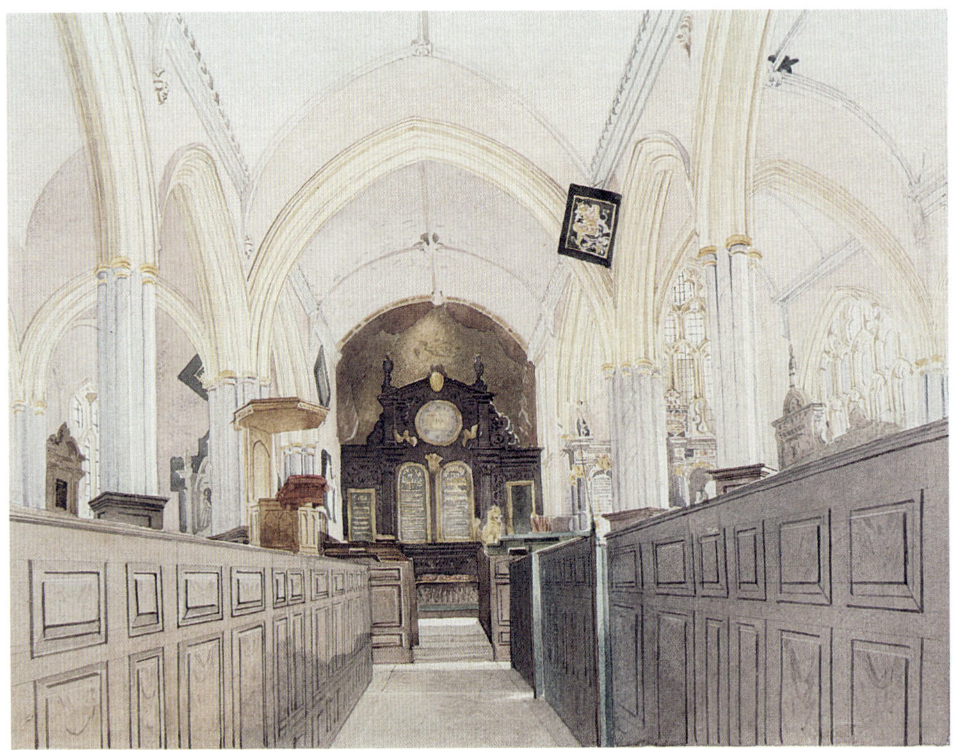

30 ***The tomb of Robert Aldworth and his wife Martha in St Peter's Church*** **1825**
Edward Cashin

Robert Aldworth was a wealthy merchant and sugar-refiner who lived in the mansion adjacent to the church, seen in the following drawings. He died in 1634 and directed that his body should lie in 'myne owne ile' in St Peter's Church.

His magnificent tomb was almost destroyed in the Blitz and then remained in the gutted church until 1958, being further damaged by the elements. Fragments are now in the Museum's collection and include the bottom panels with ships, barrels and sugar cones and pieces of the effigies.

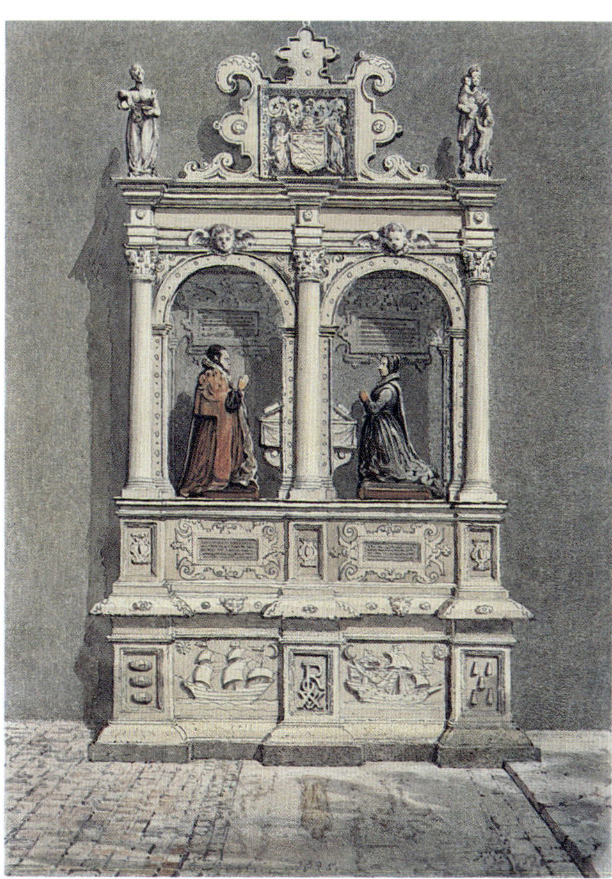

31 ***St Peter's Hospital (formerly The Mint) seen from St Peter's Churchyard*** **1821**

James Johnson

St Peter's Hospital was the finest of the timber-framed houses which Bristol once had in such abundance. It was destroyed in the Blitz, and was the greatest architectural loss of the bombing. Its site is now in Castle Park.

There had been an earlier building here, the mansion of the Norton family, which was reconstructed in 1612 by Alderman Robert Aldworth. These are the bays which faced the church and they were elaborately decorated with carved brackets, bargeboards and plasterwork. At the end of the seventeenth century the mansion was used briefly as the Bristol Mint. In 1698 it was purchased as a workhouse and administrative centre for the Bristol Incorporation of the Poor. Although renamed St Peter's Hospital, it was often still referred to as The Mint.

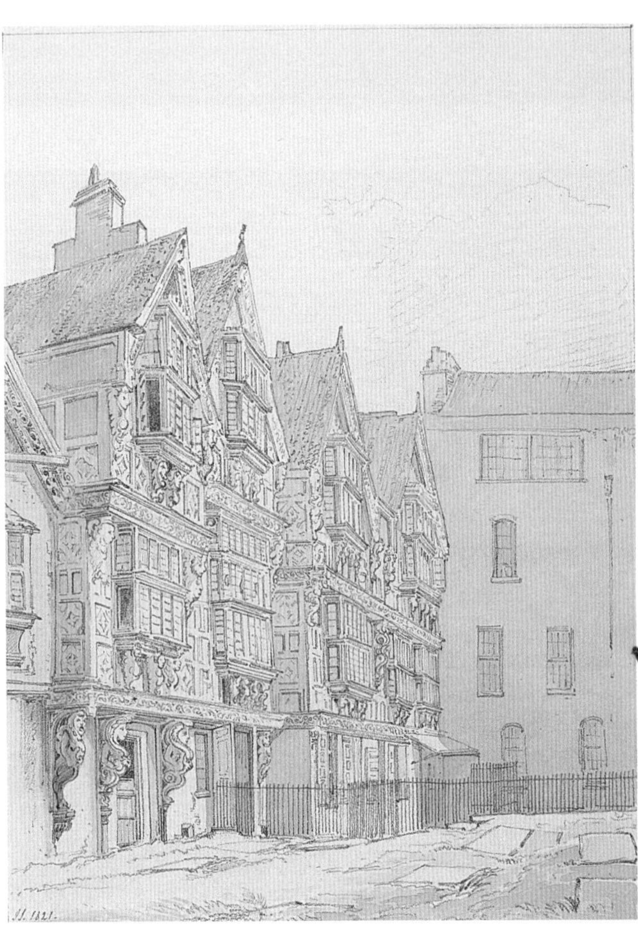

32 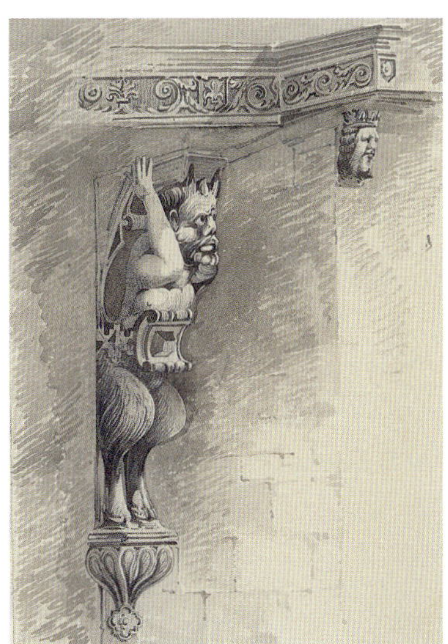

***Bracket on the façade of St Peter's Hospital* 1821**
Hugh O'Neill

Many drawings were made for Braikenridge of St Peter's Hospital including details of the façade. This was one of the grotesque corbels helping support the jettied floor above.

33 ***The back of St Peter's Hospital from the Floating Harbour* 1820**
Hugh O'Neill

This is an unusual view of St Peter's Hospital from the other side of the Floating Harbour. The back of the building was very plain and shows eighteenth-century alterations; it is unlikely that this side ever had the exuberant decoration of the front. The privies hanging over the water are a reminder of how unpleasant Bristol's harbour was. St Peter's Hospital was only a short distance above Bristol Bridge and The Back where coastal traders landed fish, fruit and other produce for the market on the quayside.

When the first cholera epidemic arrived in Bristol in the summer of 1832, St Peter's Hospital was seriously overcrowded with some 600 inmates and the disease spread rapidly through the building.

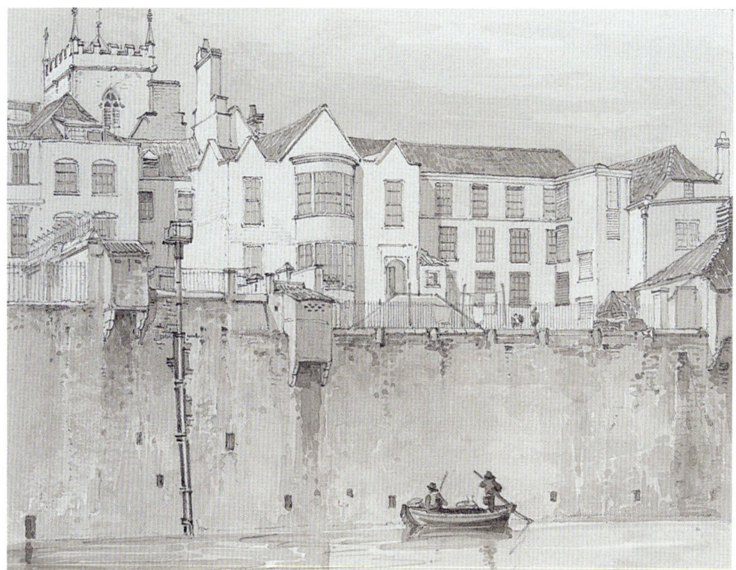

34 ***The corner of Castle Green* 1826**

Thomas L Rowbotham

In the foreground, horses pull a sledge up Castle Mill Street. Sledges with iron runners had been practical for negotiating cobbled streets and quaysides and the narrow alleys of central Bristol. Braikenridge noted that they had been falling gradually into disuse over the preceding twenty years since the introduction of four-wheeled carriages fitted with a windlass to draw up heavy casks and other goods.

Castle Green is to the left, Narrow Wine Street to the right, and ahead Bear Lane leads to Peter Street. The sign of the Cat & Wheel pub (corrupted from Catherine Wheel) is seen on the façade of the building on the left. Its corner post, with the grotesque figure, is now in the Museum's collection.

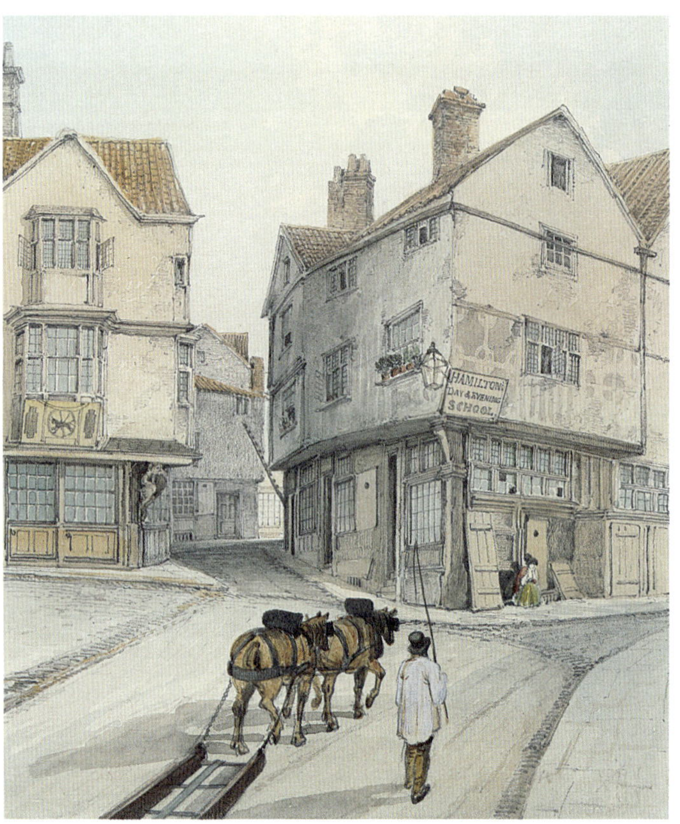

35 ***The back of Castle Green* 1820**

Hugh O'Neill

Castle Green was a street which had taken its name from the former castle. It is now a green again. The back of the street was an unusual subject and O'Neill seems to have been fascinated by the complexity of roofs and chimneys in this area of dense housing. Braikenridge noted that the artist's viewpoint was from the Mill Dam. This was the Castle Mill, a water mill which utilised the Frome for grinding corn, and O'Neill also drew it for Braikenridge. The mill was removed in 1824 and more houses erected.

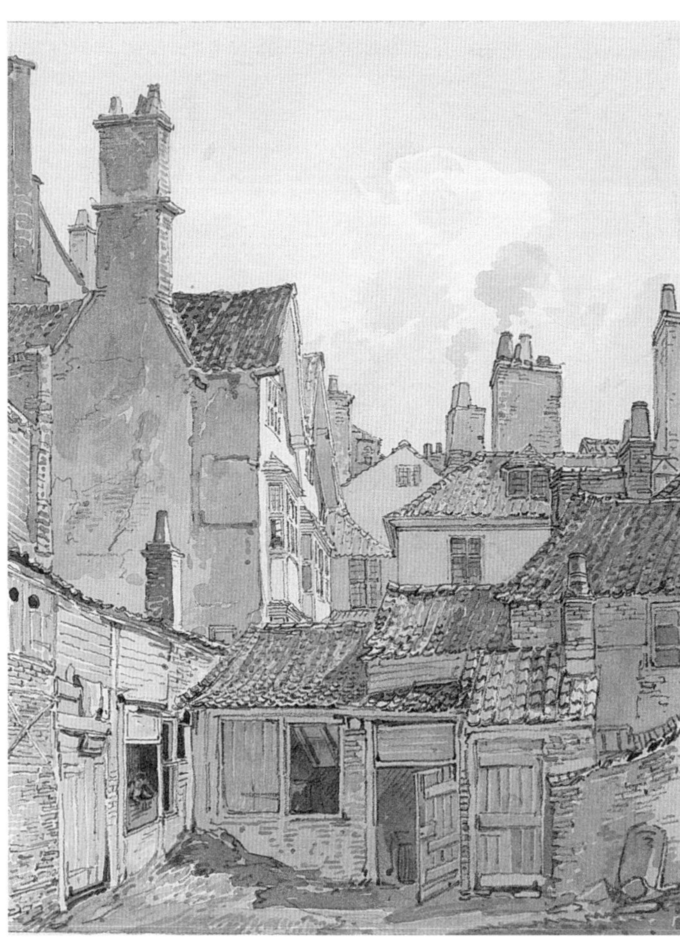

36 ***Castle Mill Street* 1825**

Thomas L Rowbotham

The topography of this area is so different today that this elevated view is difficult to imagine. Castle Mill Street descends sharply to the right to Broad Weir. The Frome flows from right to left, out of view, behind the wall near where some timber is stacked. There are industrial yards on the other bank, the large grey roof of the Ebenezer Meeting House (Methodist) in Old King Street, near the Horse Fair, and housing on the slopes of Kingsdown in the distance. The premises on the extreme right are Samuel Bedford, Artists' Colourman, at 1, Castle Green.

Braikenridge's notes on the old building were very full. He explains that the shop had not been re-let after the last occupant had moved and consequently the shutters were covered with lottery and other posters. The date on the bargeboard was difficult to make out but was either 1543 or 1547 and there were initials over the door.

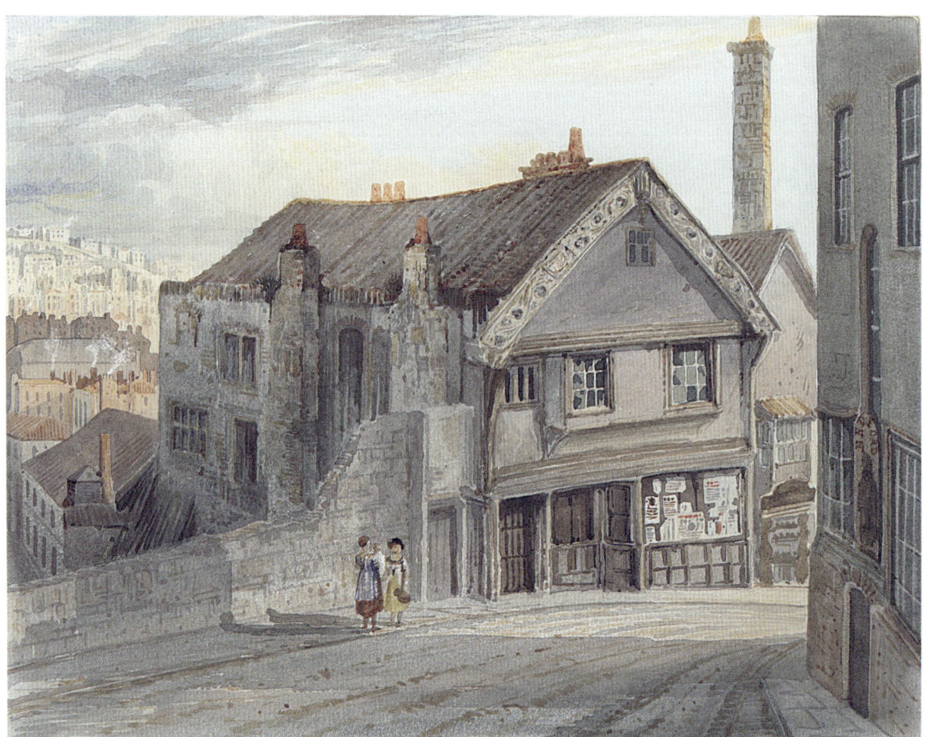

37 ***Two houses in Castle Street* 1829**

Thomas L Rowbotham

Bristol's Norman castle had been demolished on the orders of Oliver Cromwell in 1655. Castle Street was then laid out to connect Old Market to Peter Street and was the main route into Bristol from the east. These houses are dated 1663 and 1664 and therefore contemporary with the new lay-out of the castle area. They show the technique of pargetting which was a decorative moulding or incising of plaster façades. Braikenridge noted that by 1829 few examples remained in Bristol.

Castle Street was one of Bristol's fashionable shopping streets. The destruction of this area in the Blitz knocked the heart out of the city and the subsequent decision to build the replacement shopping area to its north, in Broadmead, meant a fundamental change to the topography of the historic city. In the 1970s this empty heart was laid out as a park, as previous schemes for the area had foundered through lack of resources, and in the early 1990s it was given a major revamp.

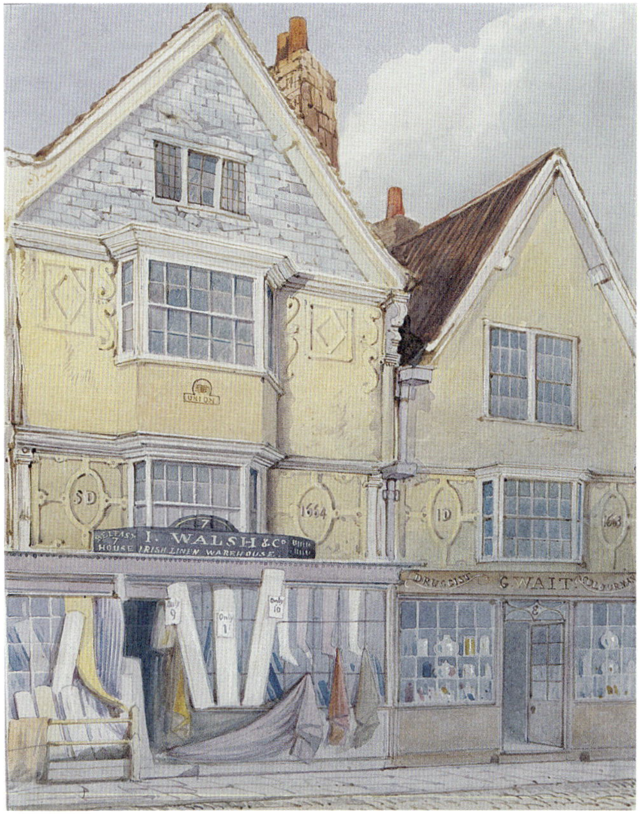

Throughout Europe, in towns and cities devastated by war, the same difficult planning decisions had to be made. There was little money to carry them out and providing homes and restoring services were a priority. In the UK, the rebuilding was modernist, for this was the brave new world. However, the rubble of Warsaw was reconstructed using early paintings as a guide and the walled town of St Malo was rebuilt in the spirit of the original. One cannot but regret that a few buildings were not salvaged from central Bristol to retain some sense of this once important part of the city.

38 ***Corner of the Horse Fair* 1821**

Hugh O'Neill

There are relatively few drawings of the area that we now call the Broadmead shopping centre in the Braikenridge Collection. It was an area of timber-framed buildings, Nonconformist meeting houses and narrow alleys and yards. The Victorians replaced many of the old buildings and it became an enchanting mixture of architecture which, although bombed in the war, had much of merit still standing afterwards.

This view is taken from St James's Churchyard, now the inner ring-road, towards (from left to right) the towers and spires of St Mary-le-Port, St Nicholas, Christ Church and All Saints.

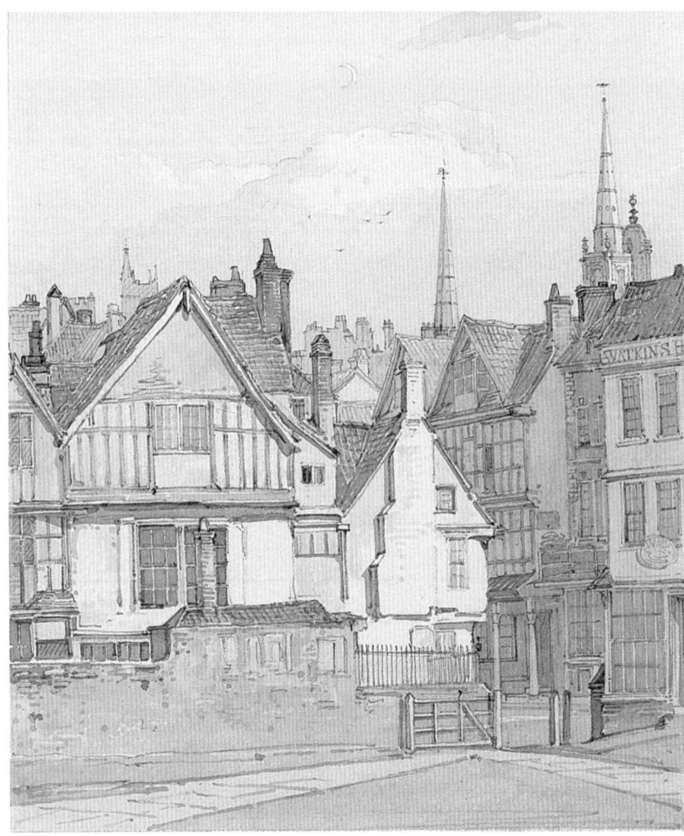

39 ***St James's Church and Silver Street* 1824**

Edward Cashin

This view looks in the opposite direction to the previous one, which was drawn from the churchyard itself. The children with the hoop are standing in the street called St James's Back (today's Silver Street) and on the left is the White Horse Inn on the corner of Bridewell Lane. The ladies stand by a butcher's shop, where a carcass hangs outside. Silver Street leads off behind them towards Lower Maudlin Lane. The shop in the centre on the Horse Fair, behind the gas street lamp, carries a sign advertising George Cox's pottery. His stoneware pottery was made in Avon Street, St Philip's. On the right a barber's pole is outside the hair-dressing business of William Hicks.

The information provided by drawings in the Braikenridge Collection, together with *Mathews' Bristol Directory* and John Plumley and George Ashmead's great map of the city, published in 1829, enables a detailed picture to be built up of vanished areas of the city.

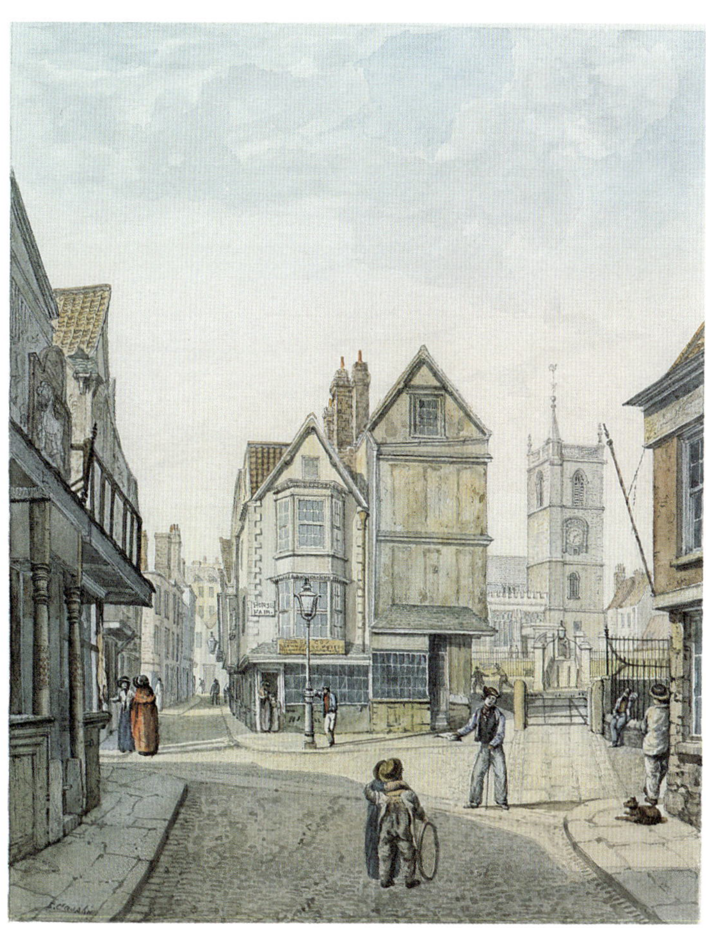

40 ***St Philip's Church and Narrow Plain* 1828**

Thomas L Rowbotham

The artist stood in Passage Street, with Tower Hill off to the left and Narrow Plain in the shadow to the right of the figures. All of the street names remain today but without SS Philip and James's Church (Pip'n Jay) the view would be unrecognisable. The houses have been replaced with modern office blocks and the Central Health Clinic stands on the corner on the left.

The Temple Back Ferry across the Floating Harbour from Counterslip landed at Passage Street. St Philip's Bridge replaced the ferry in 1838, which had been carrying over 100,000 passengers a year.

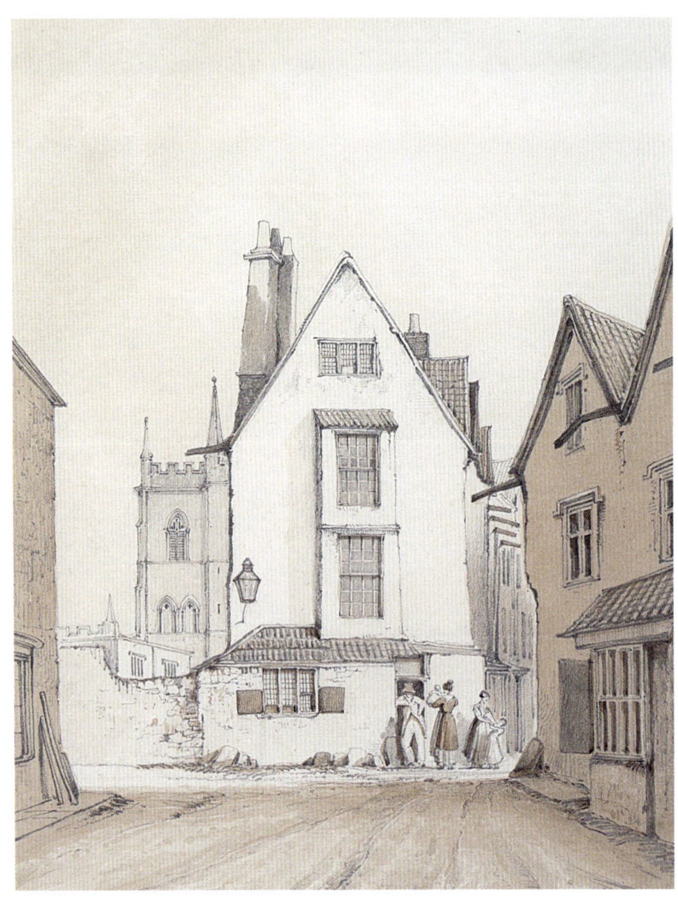

41 ***Entrance to the Piepoudre Court, Old Market*** **1822**

Hugh O'Neill

Old Market was Bristol's oldest market, held in the street to the east of the castle. The Court of Piepoudre (pieds poudrés: dusty feet) existed from the thirteenth century and sat to adjudicate over market issues. In later centuries it sat in the buildings shown here. Braikenridge noted that the entrance to the court was between the pillars of the central house. However, it is now the building on the right, the Stag and Hounds pub, which is associated with the court although it clearly once utilised more buildings. His notes continue 'The Court of Pied Poudre continues to be opened there every first of October & the sittings are held for 8 days. The sort of refreshment taken by the Members of the Corporation who officiate before they proceed to business viz Toasted Cheese & metheglin marks the antiquity of this branch of civic jurisdiction.' Metheglin was a medieval beverage made from honey and herbs. Beer and cider were also distributed to the populace and the resultant rowdiness caused the court to be suppressed after 1870.

By the 1970s Old Market had fallen into dereliction. It escaped destruction and has been rescued, though slowly, and its dislocation from the main city is symptomatic of Bristol's planning problems. The ring-roads constructed in the 1950s and 1960s were made when engineering was more important than old buildings and conservation was of little interest. The new roads isolated areas like Old Market and destroyed much of the city's character. It is a challenge for the future to integrate these areas again and minimise the scars of fly-overs and roundabouts.

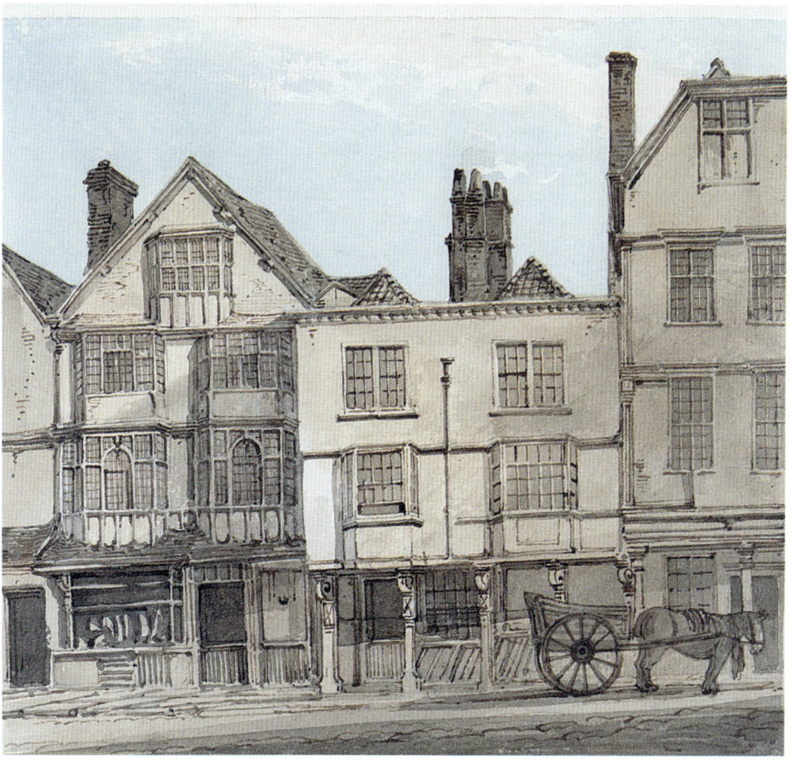

THE FROME FROM BROAD WEIR TO ST AUGUSTINE'S REACH

42 ***Tabernacle Bridge* 1821**

Hugh O'Neill

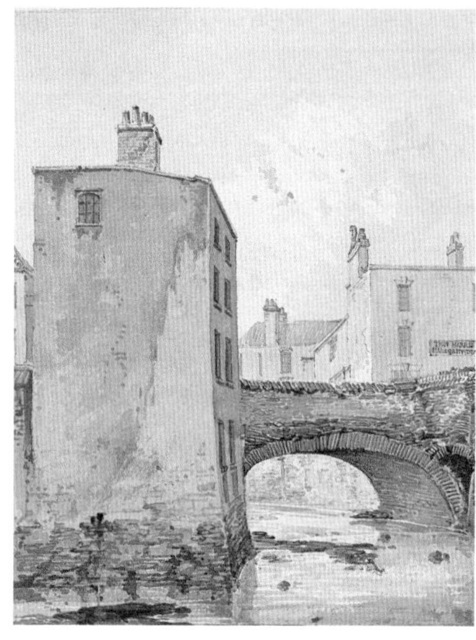

The River Frome is now culverted for much of its course through the city but in Braikenridge's time it was open. He died in 1856 and it was in the following year that the Council began the long process of arching over the river, a section at a time. A short stretch of water can be seen today between the end of the M32 and Wade Street and it then disappears beneath the city to re-emerge at St Augustine's Reach.

This drawing looks downstream towards the centre of Bristol. The Tabernacle was a Nonconformist Meeting House in Penn Street, which was to the right of this bridge, and the signboard advertises mahogany at Thomas Harris', the timber merchant. Although the bridge looks decrepit, Braikenridge wrote 'The arch has been in this state for many years & is quite firm'. Although the name of Penn Street was retained when the Broadmead shopping centre was laid out it is not in the same position as the original street. The location of Tabernacle Bridge is therefore under the south side of Philadelphia Court, the entrance to a car park on the east side of modern Penn Street. It is just north of a Pizza Hut.

The drawings of the Frome are more attractive than the reality of Bristol in the 1820s. Sewage and industrial waste were dumped in the river and then flowed into the Floating Harbour. As the construction of the harbour meant that it was no longer flushed with the tides the pollution and smell built up to often unbearable levels, particularly in warm weather.

43 ***Broad Weir* 1821**

Hugh O'Neill

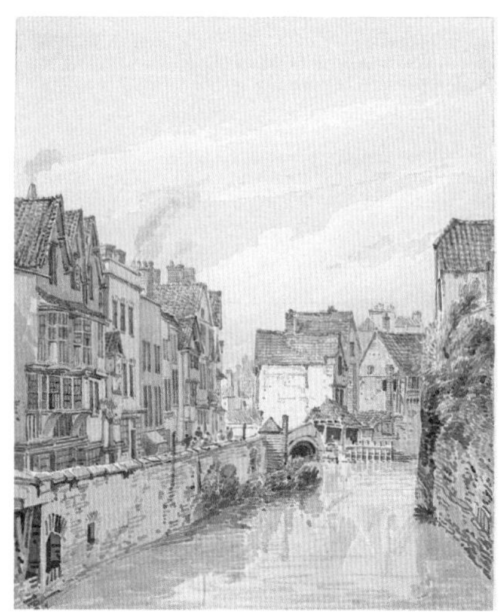

The street on the left is Broad Weir and this is the section of the Frome which had once formed part of the castle moat. The arch seen on the left at the end of this stretch of water leads to Narrow Weir and the upstream continuation of the Frome; the moat also continued to the right along a section known as Castle Ditch. The moat can be seen today where it joins the Floating Harbour at the Castle Park end of Queen Street, near the ambulance station.

44 ***The entrance to the Pithay from Union Street* 1823**

James Johnson

This is a particularly difficult view to envisage today. It is taken from the bridge on Union Street; the steps descended to a lane leading to the Pithay. Today we would be standing with our backs to The Galleries shopping mall and looking down onto Fairfax Street, which has covered the waters of the Frome here since about 1860. The spire of St John-on-the-Wall is now concealed by tower blocks and this is an ugly section of modern Bristol.

The house beneath the spire, overhanging the river, is built on the remains of a bastion which can be seen at water level. This would have been a defence on the second, outer wall of the medieval town, which ran from Newgate to the bottom of Small Street. Several other drawings in the collection show the remains of these defences along the Frome. A recent archaeological excavation on the other bank here, behind the high wall in the right foreground, discovered a substantial early medieval house.

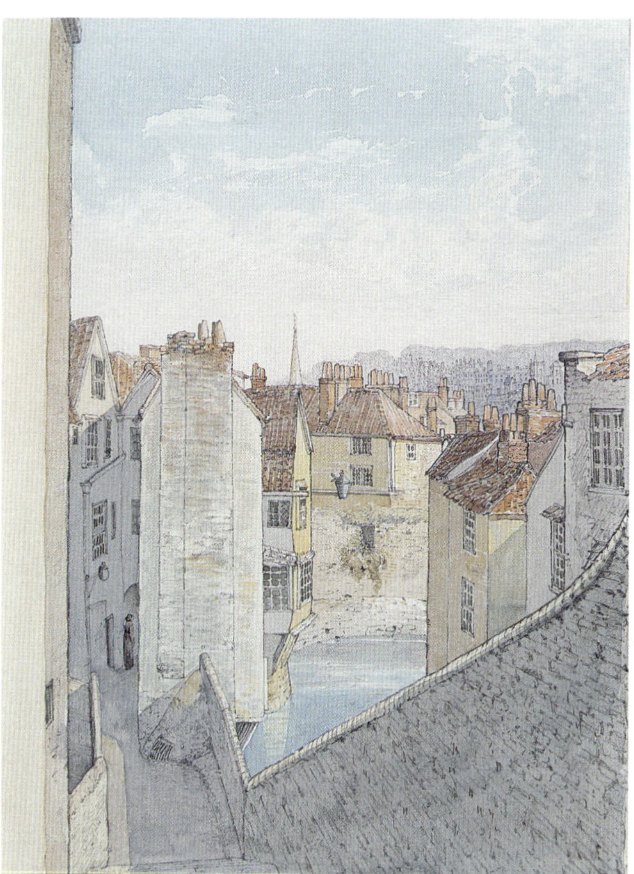

45 ***Bridewell Bridge seen through the prison gates* 1824**
Edward Cashin

Two fashionable ladies are talking together on the bridge, the waters of the Frome running beneath their feet. We are looking at them from the section of Bridewell Lane that ran through the prison and these are the gates which the mob were to throw into the river during the 1831 Riots. Conditions in the prison were appalling, with open sewers and numerous rats. The site later became the central police station.

The business on the other side of the river is Joseph Mathews Taylor's, a boot and shoemaker. The spirelet on the tower of St James's Church can just be seen above the rooftops.

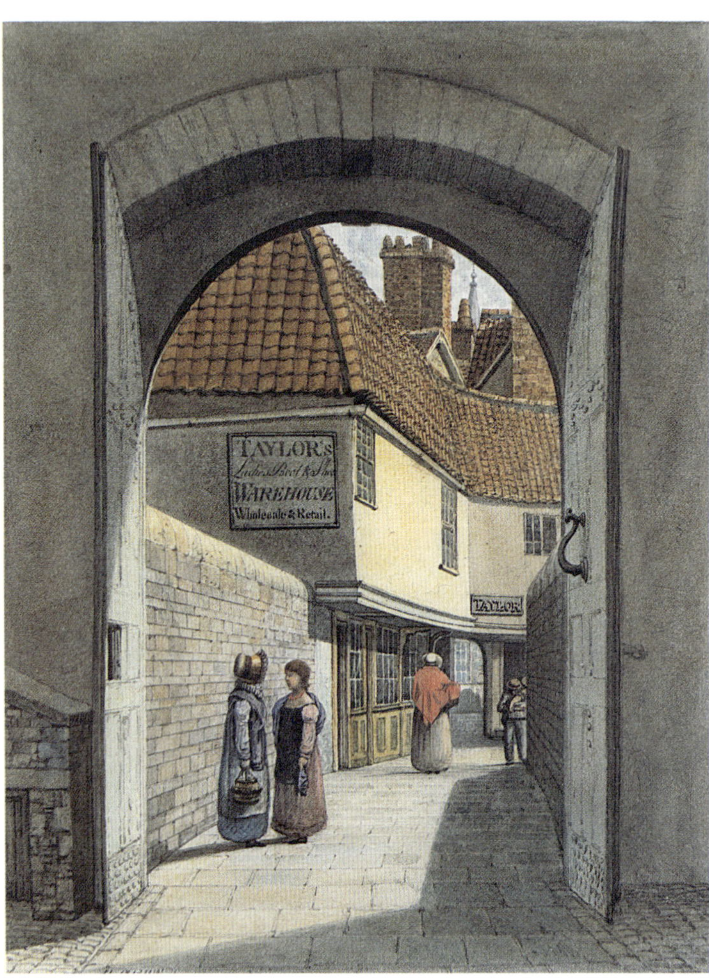

46 ***St James's Back* 1820**

Hugh O'Neill

One section of the street called St James's Back ran north towards the Horse Fair from the junction of Broadmead with Nelson Street; it is today's Silver Street. This drawing is of the backs of the houses, overlooking the Frome. It is a typical image of the ramshackle housing that was in the area. During the1820s, the population of Bristol and its suburbs increased to 100,000 and the slums in the central area were overcrowded. The toll of the cholera epidemics of the next decades was concentrated in these poorer, filthy areas of the city.

This section of the river was one of the last to be covered over in the centre of the city and the work was done in the late 1860s.

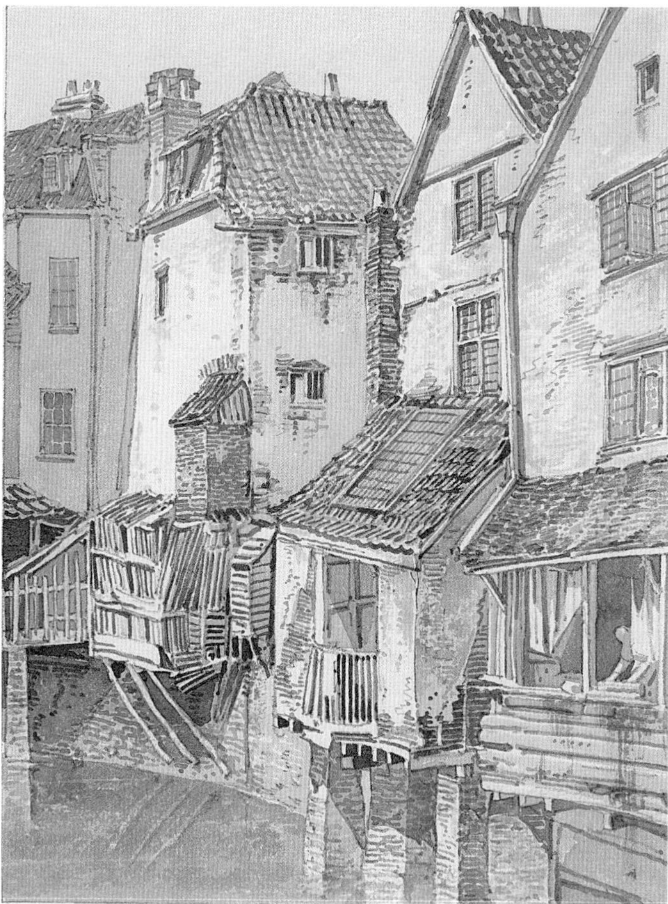

47 ***Old houses in Lewin's Mead with the Adam & Eve public house* 1810**

Hugh O'Neill

This is another example of the varied street architecture that once characterised central Bristol. The buildings here cover at least 300 years, from the sixteenth to the eighteenth centuries, including multi-jettied timber-fronted houses. The Adam & Eve was entered under the signboard; the view from its back room is shown in the drawing opposite. When Braikenridge first met O'Neill in 1820 he bought a few drawings that the artist had made before he lived in Bristol; this one was drawn in 1810.

Bristol's great historian, John Latimer, wrote of Lewin's Mead that by the middle of the nineteenth century it was 'notorious for the degraded character of its inhabitants'. However, in previous centuries it had been a respectable residential area for merchants. They then moved out to pleasant Georgian suburbs to escape the pollution of the centre of the city.

The decline of Lewin's Mead's continued for another century and it is now, visually, a bleak area of the city where large office blocks sit tightly against the inner circuit road. Their poor architectural quality is typical of the speculative development of the late 1960s and early 1970s. Recently, between those blocks and Christmas Steps, there has been inspired regeneration of both the Unitarian Chapel and a sugar house (refinery) which have been converted for modern use.

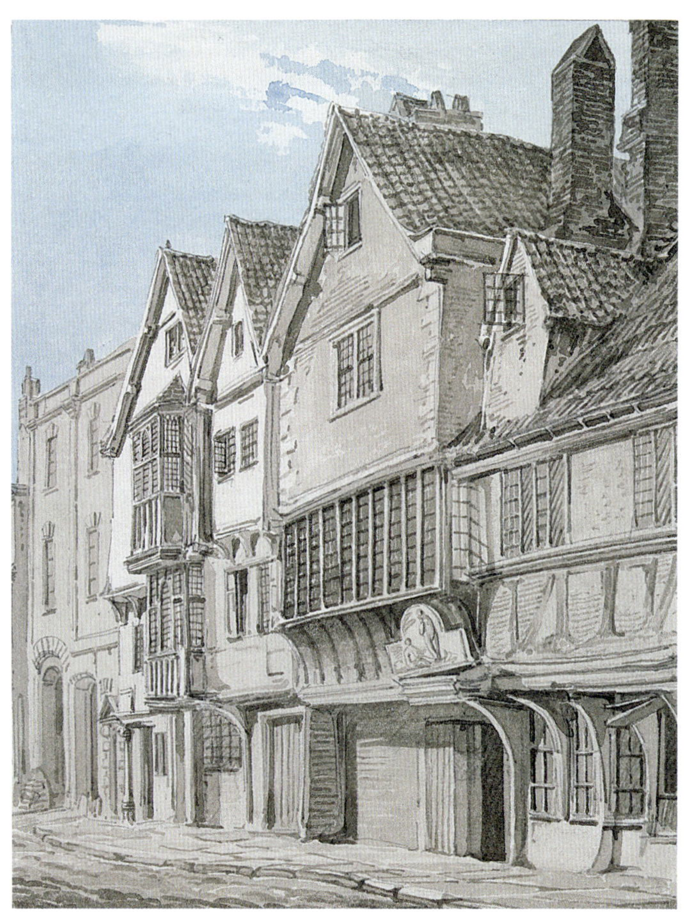

48 ***St John's Bridge seen from the back of the Adam & Eve, Lewin's Mead*** **1821**

Hugh O'Neill

We are looking down the Frome and the densely packed housing above the bridge is at the bottom of St Michael's Hill (the top of today's Colston Street). The next bridge downstream was Christmas Street Bridge and a part of it, and its reflection, can be glimpsed under St John's Bridge.

It was not so picturesque as it appears as privies hung over the river and industrial premises also discharged pollutants into the water. Nevertheless, the lower reaches of the Floating Harbour were a popular bathing spot for boys and men, oblivious to the health risks. The Royal Commission report on public health in large urban areas, published in 1845, was to show that the high mortality rates in Bristol were directly attributable to the filthy state of the city. However, it wasn't until the mid-1850s that work at last began on installing a system of sewers.

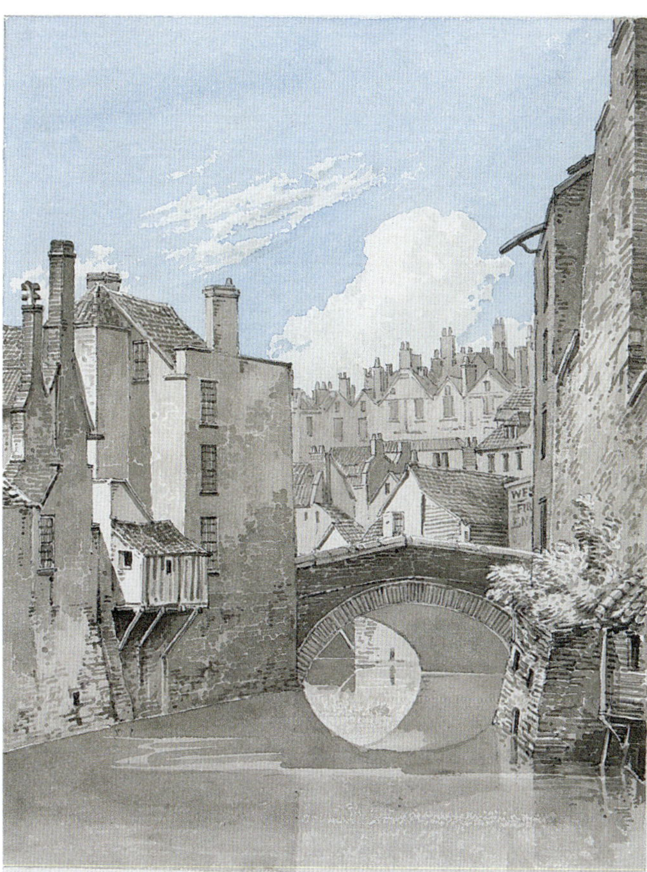

49 ***The Stone Bridge, at the Head of the Quay* 1825**

Thomas L Rowbotham

Formerly called St Giles's Bridge, the Stone Bridge was the highest navigable point of the Frome. This section of the harbour was used by the Severn trows (flat-bottomed barges). Although this stretch of the river is now covered over, the structure of the bridge remains intact beneath the capping.

The church is St Michael's and the large building to its right is the Host Street sugar house where raw or semi-refined sugar imported from the Caribbean and America was refined into white sugar. Sugar had been refined in Bristol from the early seventeenth century and was an important industry, particularly in the eighteenth century. The last sugar house closed in 1912.

The business on the left was John Willis, Cabinetmaker, Upholsterer and Undertaker. Northcliffe House, a fine Art Deco building of circa 1929, is now on the site and is about to be restored and refurbished as offices.

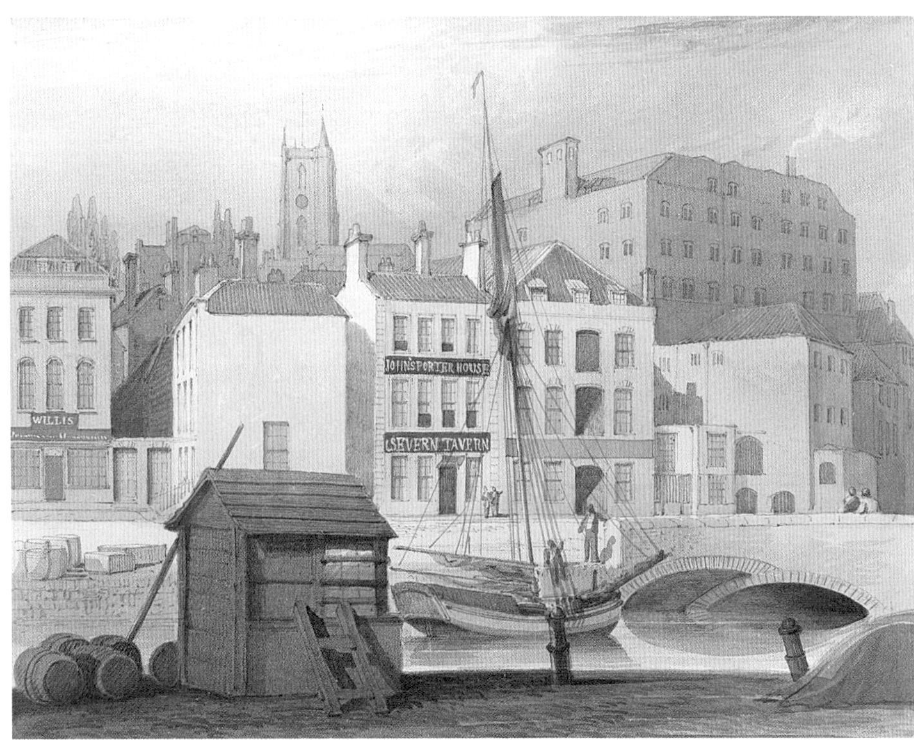

50 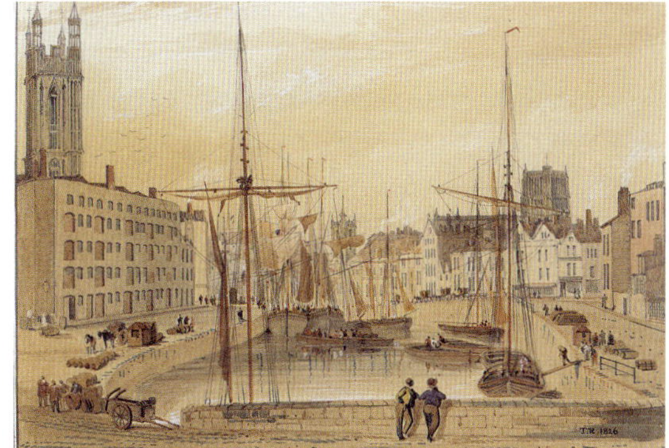

View from the Stone Bridge 1826

Thomas L Rowbotham

The view looks towards St Augustine's Reach from the Quay Head at Stone Bridge. It was the head of Bristol's medieval harbour. The Frome had originally run east from near here and it joined the Avon below Bristol Bridge. In the middle of the thirteenth century a great channel was dug to divert the Frome and make a fine harbour which joined the Avon at today's Arnolfini gallery. The largest ships of the time could be accommodated and they rested on soft mud at low tide.

In front of St Stephen's Church are the tontine warehouses, built at the end of the eighteenth century. A tontine was a speculative investment which was more like a lottery. In 1783 money was put up by 195 people to complete the warehouses, according to the tontine principle. The principle is that the proceeds are eventually divided amongst the surviving investors, some of whom will have died, and - it is said - will have died in mysterious circumstances!

This section of the Frome was to be covered over in the 1890s, having been a harbour since the 1240s. The space was now needed for trams and became known as the The Tramways Centre. As ever, the name endured longer than the function, and it is still known as the Centre.

51 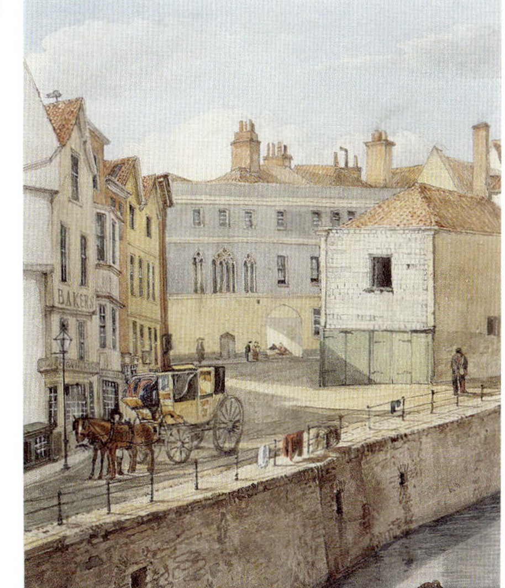

Lady Huntingdon's Chapel seen from the Drawbridge 1824

George W Delamotte

The view is towards what is now the bottom of Colston Street, where the late Lady Huntingdon had converted an older building into a chapel in 1775. The chapel is in the centre, with three Gothic windows, and Church of England services were conducted here according to Lady Huntingdon's format. Later in the nineteenth century it was used as a Salvation Army Hall. The distinctive yellow coach is a hackney cab standing at the end of its rank by the Drawbridge.

Colston House, a stylish 1930s building, is now on the site of the chapel. Some of the buildings on the left survive and were restored in a very successful scheme of the 1980s to restore the corner of St Augustine's Parade and Place and integrate sympathetic new buildings. The Braikenridge Collection can be a valuable source of information for such urban conservation projects.

52 ***The Drawbridge and part of the Frome* 1826**

Thomas L Rowbotham

St Augustine's Bridge, usually known as the Drawbridge (from its construction) crossed the Frome near the end of Clare Street. There were frequent delays and disruptions for traffic when the bridge was drawn back to allow small coastal vessels to pass. The steam packet agent was on the corner of Broad Quay and Braikenridge tells us that his large signboard had been painted recently. Steam packets to Ireland from Bristol had been introduced in the early 1820s and the thirty hours to Cork was a huge improvement on the old service which could, at its worst, take weeks. To the right of the packet office is the column at Dial Slip, Broad Quay. On the opposite side of St Augustine's Reach, to the right of the ships drying their sails, a signal flag flies on a small tower (see plate 54). The church is St Augustine-the-Less and on the far right there is a rank of hackney cabs.

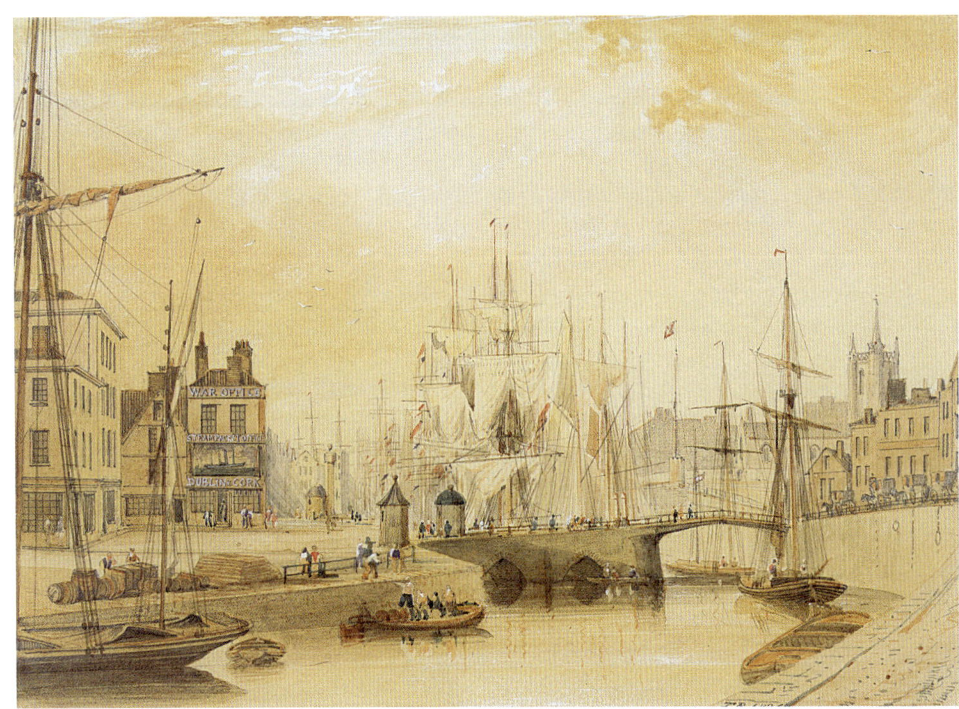

53 ***Cleaning the Floating Harbour* 1828**

Thomas L Rowbotham

This drawing is a reminder of what the harbour must have looked like when it was tidal, before the construction of the permanent high tide of the Floating Harbour in 1809. The quaysides of the Floating Harbour were prone to silting up and, in order to shift the mud, first the harbour was drained by opening the lock gates. That draining has already happened here and a vessel is shown placed across the water of the River Frome to channel its flow. About a hundred men with shovels then loosened the mud and the river carried it away. St Michael's Church is in the background, rising above the Great House, then home to Colston's School and now the site of Colston Hall.

This was the final section of the Frome to be covered over and work started in 1937. The capping ran from the bridge shown here (originally the Drawbridge, later replaced with a fixed bridge) to the top of Narrow Quay and was in preparation for the construction of Redcliffe Way and its junction with the Centre. The new road was constructed diagonally across Queen Square and mutilated it, but this has now been rectified in a restoration scheme. After that restoration success, many Bristolians feel today that an opportunity has been missed in not opening up the water again in the recently remodelled City Centre.

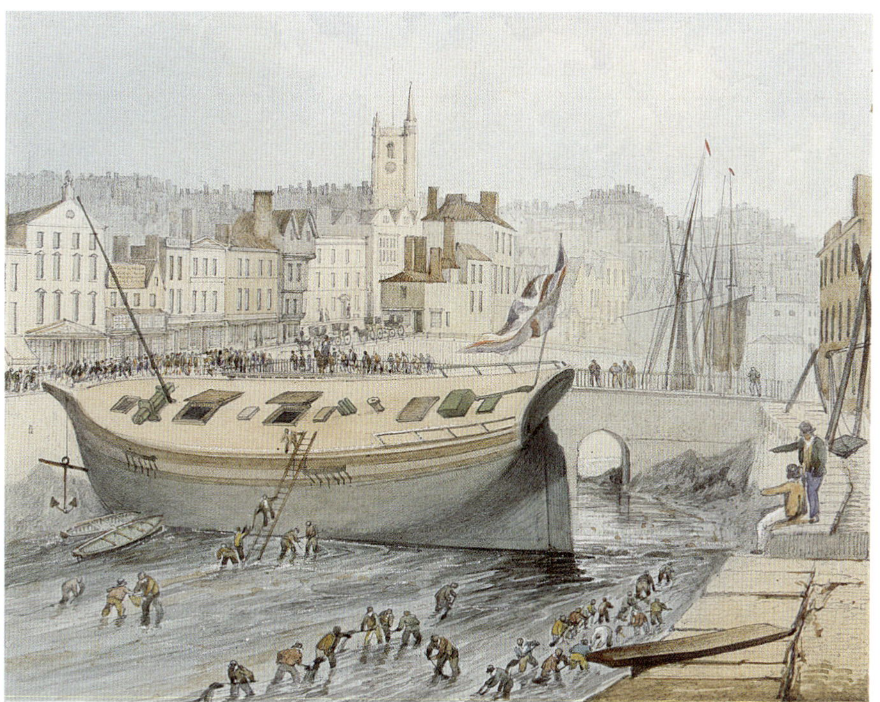

54 ***St Augustine's Back*** **1824**

Hugh O'Neill

We are on Broad Quay, looking across St Augustine's Reach to an area called The Butts. The church is St Augustine-the-Less. It was a parish church on College Green related to St Augustine's Abbey, which had become the Cathedral from 1542. The church was slightly damaged during the Second World War, neglected afterwards and finally demolished in 1962.

On the right, barely distinguishable in the tangle of rigging, is a flag-staff mounted on a small crenellated tower. Braikenridge variously called this the signal flag-staff for the Water Bailiff or the Quay Warden. These were two separate officials and, as their titles suggest, one ensured the water of the Floating Harbour was properly managed for shipping and the other managed the quaysides. Later in the century the flag-staff was removed and the building was used as a gents' urinal.

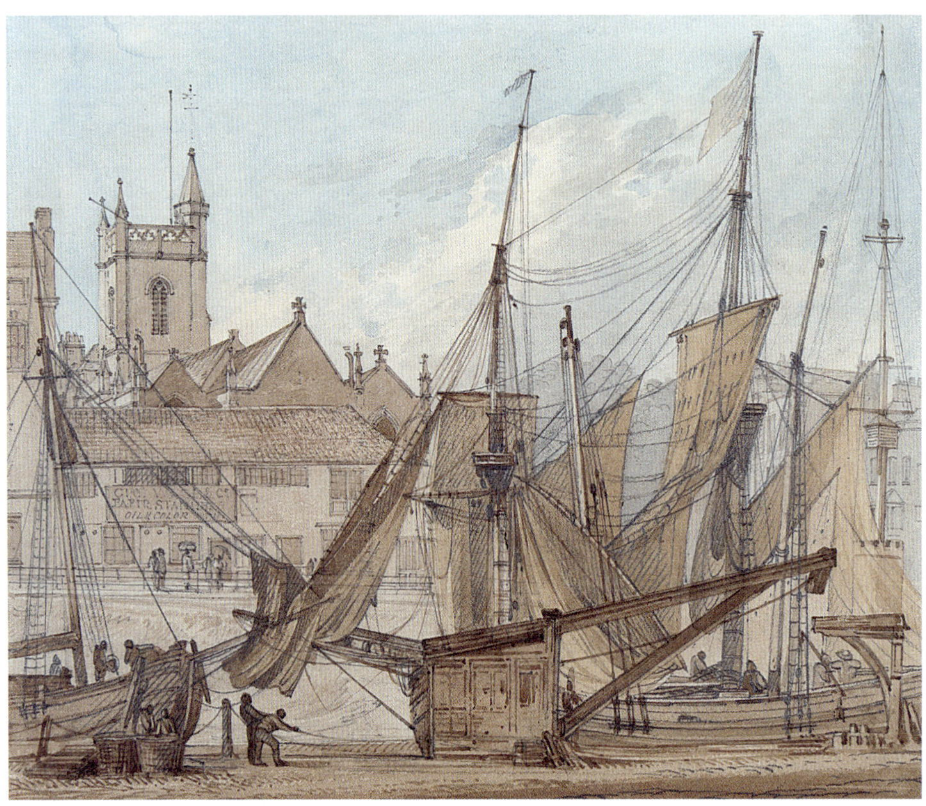

55 ***The Butts* 1826**

Edward Cashin

This is on the site of today's Watershed Media Centre, looking towards the Cathedral. Trinity Street is just in front of the tower. The yard was that of Protheroe & Brown, dealers in mahogany, deal and other timber.

Braikenridge's catalogue noted a recent change: 'Since this drawing was made the Door at the end of the old House has been closed up & re-opened in the front which has much injured the appearance of it'.

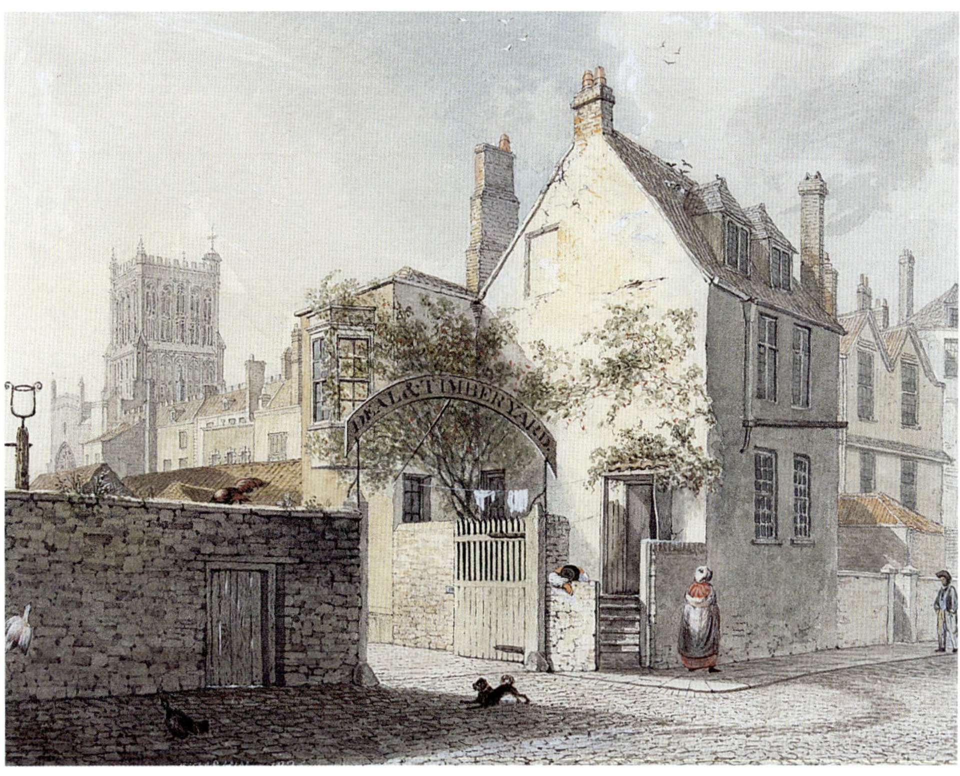

NORTHERN ASPECTS

56 ***North view of Bristol Cathedral*** **1824**

Samuel Jackson

The imposing mass of the Cathedral's central tower was completed in the late fifteenth century. However, for 400 years the building looked very different than it does today as it was not until later in the nineteenth century that George Edmund Street added the nave and west towers. Before that, there was a blank wall at the west end and, as can be seen here, buildings were constructed against it. These were removed about ten years after this drawing was made to improve the appearance of the Cathedral.

There are a large number of drawings of ecclesiastical subjects in the Braikenridge Collection: interior views, architectural details, monuments, stained glass and so on. They are an important record of the pre-Victorian appearance of Bristol's churches.

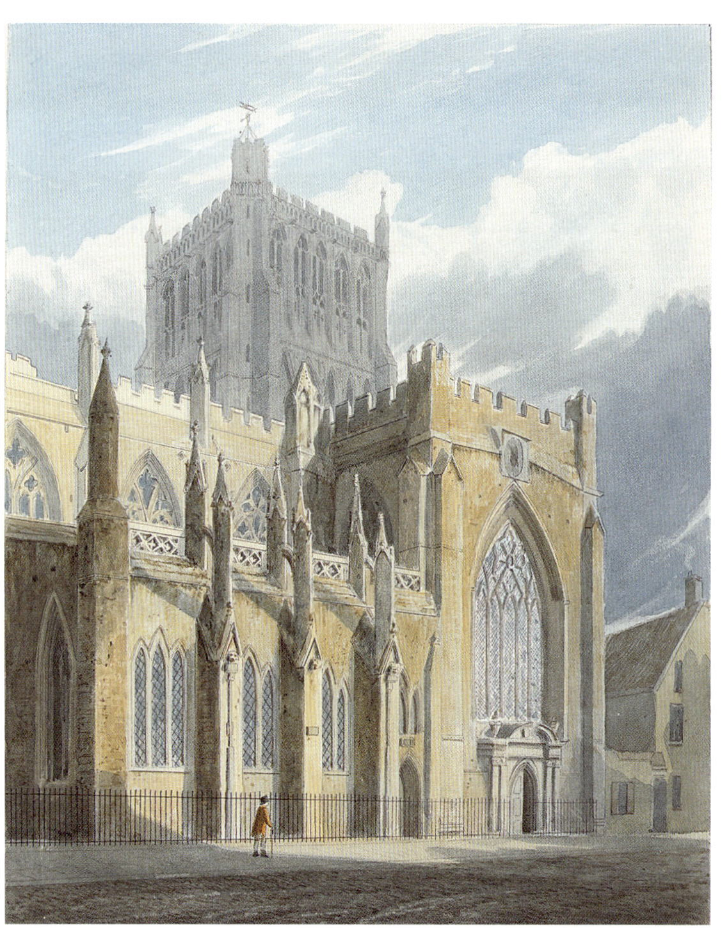

57 ***St Mark's, the Mayor's Chapel, with a view up Park Street* c. 1826**

Thomas L Rowbotham

St Mark's is the only civic church in the country and the chapel had originally served the Hospital of the Gaunts. It was surrendered at the Dissolution and purchased by the Council in 1541. It was not called the Lord Mayor's Chapel until 1899, when the office of mayor was elevated by Queen Victoria. The construction of the current Council House in the mid-twentieth century brought the two civic buildings into a happy proximity.

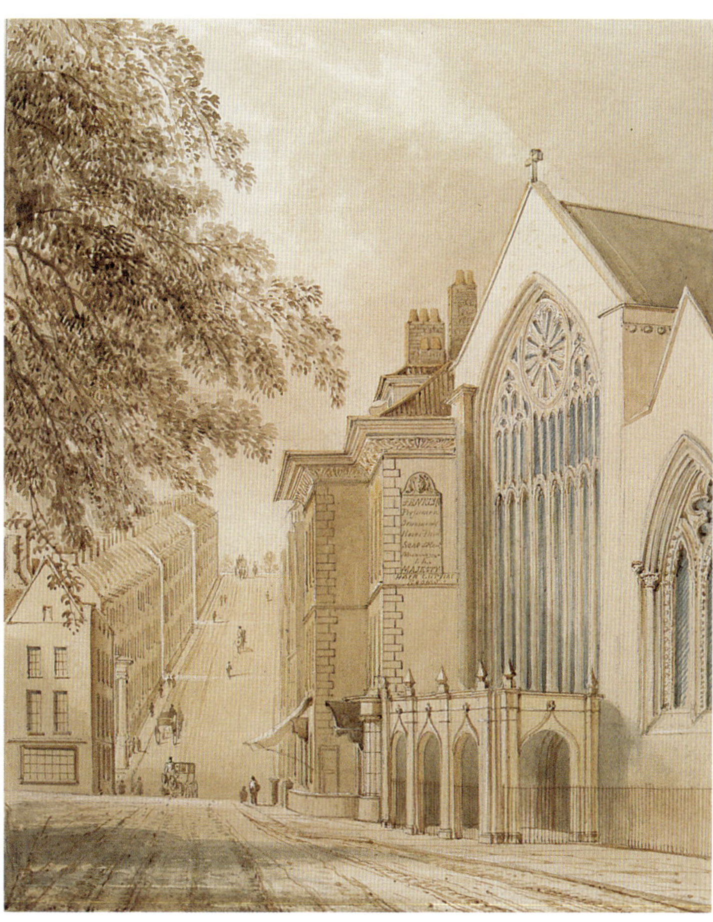

The Gothick church porch shown here was added in the late 1770s. The sign on the wall above it is for John Franklyn, listed in the street directory as 'Perfumer, Ornamental hair, and Botanic oil manufacturer to his Majesty, and Medicine vender'. His premises were in a house built in about 1700.

The great west window is not the original for there were substantial restorations at the chapel in the 1820s. The window was removed and a copy installed while the original was purchased by Henry Brooke of Henbury Hill House who, in Braikenridge's words, 'set it up in a sham ruin on Henbury Hill to serve as an object from his house' to be immediately dubbed 'Brooke's Folly' by the local people. It still exists today, off the Ridgeway, very close to modern housing.

Park Street was altered later in the century and the hollow at its junction with Frog Lane and Frogmore Street was bridged to improve the gradient. This had been anticipated when Park Street was first laid out and the houses at the bottom had high basements and flights of steps.

58 ***The Cathedral and College Green from Great George Street* 1827**

Thomas L Rowbotham

The artist's vantage point was in Great George Street where there was a substantial plot of land that had not been built upon. It was later filled with a Victorian terrace. The Council House is now on the site of the row of gabled houses, centre right, and the brightly lit street in the centre is College Place, which linked College Street with the Green. Braikenridge did not record the reason why the churches were flying flags.

In the distance, the masts of ships can be seen in the harbour. The green hills are Pile Hill on the left, with the small cluster of buildings at Totterdown, and Windmill Hill to its right.

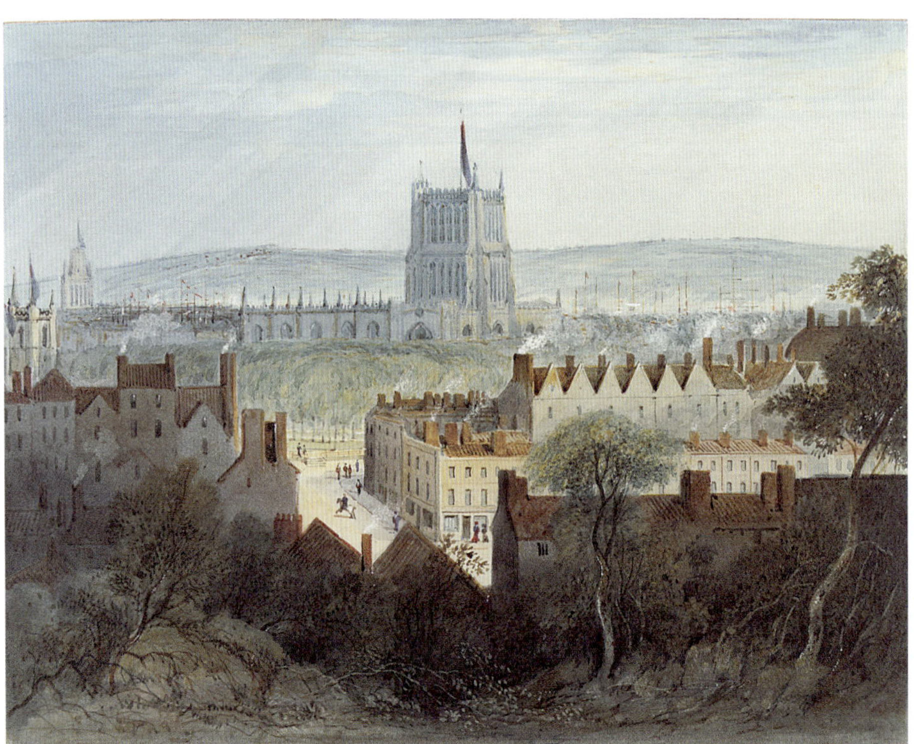

59 ***St George's Church, Great George Street* 1824**

Edward Cashin

St George's was completed in 1823, the same year that its architect, Robert Smirke, began his designs for the British Museum. It was a Commissioners' church, paid for from the sum of one million pounds set aside by Act of Parliament in 1818 for the building of churches in newly populous places. It served the fast-developing area around Brandon Hill and Park Street (which had been laid out in the 1760s) and was designed in the new Greek Revival style.

Before the new church was built, seven unfinished houses on the site had to be knocked down. They had been started during the speculative building boom in the late eighteenth century, which had crashed on the outbreak of war with France in 1793. There were other houses in the area in the same ruinous state, as in the other Georgian suburbs. Robert Southey wrote of Clifton, 'Here too, as well as at Bath, is the dismal sight of streets and crescents which have never been finished, the most dolorous of all ruins' (*Letters from England*, 1807). It was estimated that over 500 houses in Bristol were left unfinished and it was many years before they were completed.

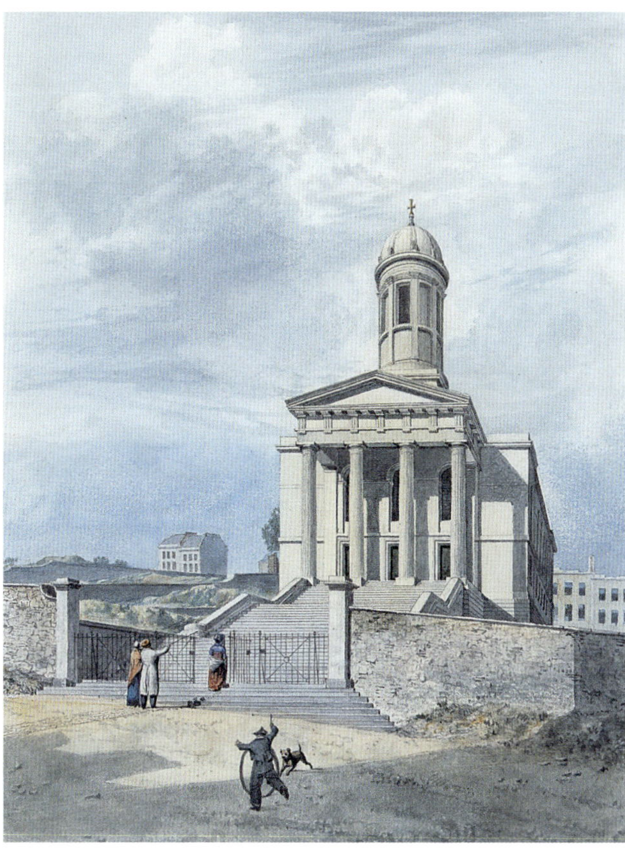

60 ***View of Bristol from below the Royal Fort, Tyndall's Park, with Evan Baillie's house* 1825**

Samuel Jackson

This sloping parkland is now covered by University of Bristol buildings and Woodland Road. The large Georgian house belonged to Evan Baillie, a wealthy banker. It was later replaced by the Prince's Theatre in Park Row and a petrol station is now on the site.

Almost hidden by trees on the left is a garden gazebo in the grounds of a villa once belonging to the eighteenth-century alderman and merchant, Henry Muggleworth. He lived here in the summer and early autumn to escape from his Lewin's Mead house near the malodorous Frome.

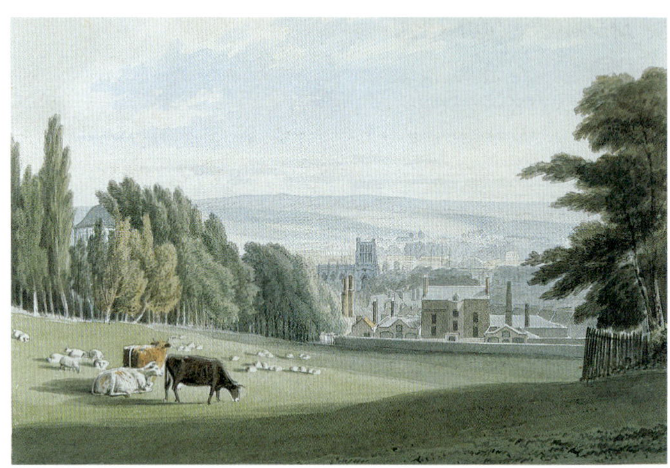

61 

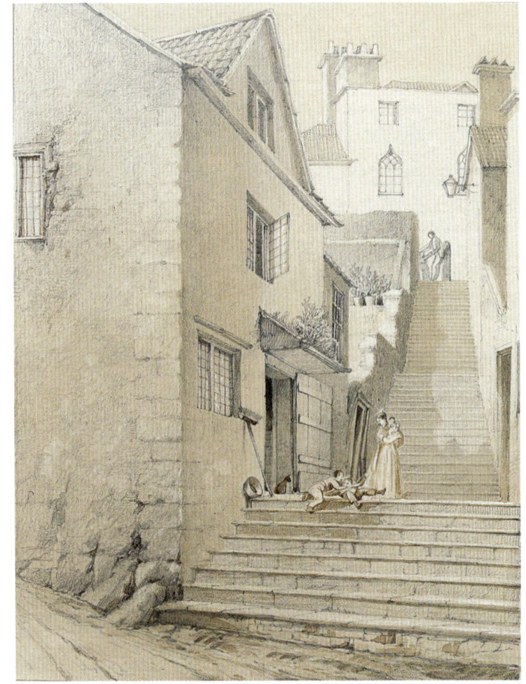

***The steps connecting Griffin Lane and Church Lane* 1828**

Thomas L Rowbotham

This area changed dramatically when Perry Road and Colston Street were laid out later in the century. Many old houses were demolished and the street pattern was changed. These steps connected the lower level at Griffin Lane (now Lower Park Row) with Church Lane (Lower Church Lane). On Plumley and Ashmead's map of the city they are simply called Bristol Steps and should not be confused with the upper section of Christmas Steps. Perry Road was laid through the middle of this area.

62 ***St Michael's Hill* 1828**

Thomas L Rowbotham

St Michael's Hill is still one of the most attractive streets in Bristol although these seventeenth-century houses near the bottom were demolished for the construction of Perry Road, opened in 1868. The distinctive, bulbous pillars date their construction to after the Civil War. Note the parrot in a cage near the left pillar.

In the early 1970s parts of St Michael's Hill were again under threat, both from the expansion of the hospitals and the insatiable desire for road-widening. However, pressure from amenity groups, particularly the Kingsdown Conservation Group, prevented further demolition.

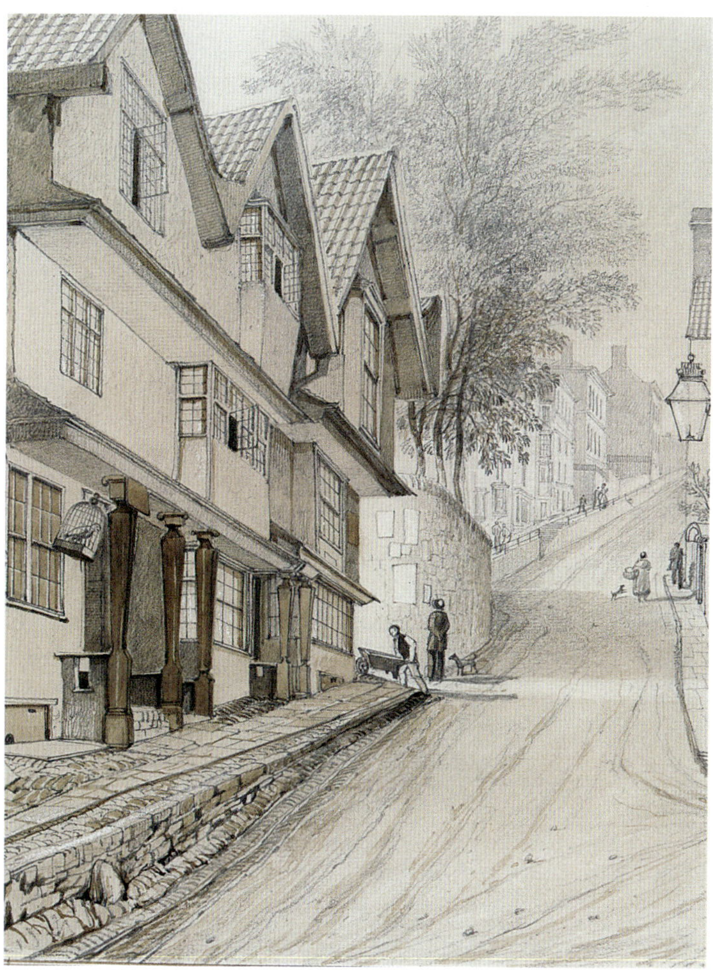

63 ***View from the top of Lodge Street* 1826**

Thomas L Rowbotham

Lodge Street, which still retains its cobble stones, was laid out in the 1780s and named after the Red Lodge. The wall on the right is the Red Lodge's garden wall and the door above the child is still the door into the garden. The Red Lodge was built about 1590 in the grounds of the Great House, seen here at the bottom of the street. At the time of this drawing the Great House was Colston's School for boys, which was noted for producing good accountants. Colston Hall now stands on its site.

The left-hand side of Lodge Street also survives, including the porch on the left. The street had been allowed to fall into dereliction in the mid-twentieth century but was restored in the 1980s. This was a triumph for the Bristol Churches Housing Association and the conservation-led planning of the final decades of the century. The right-hand side of the street is gone, and the restored houses look across to an ugly multi-storey car-park.

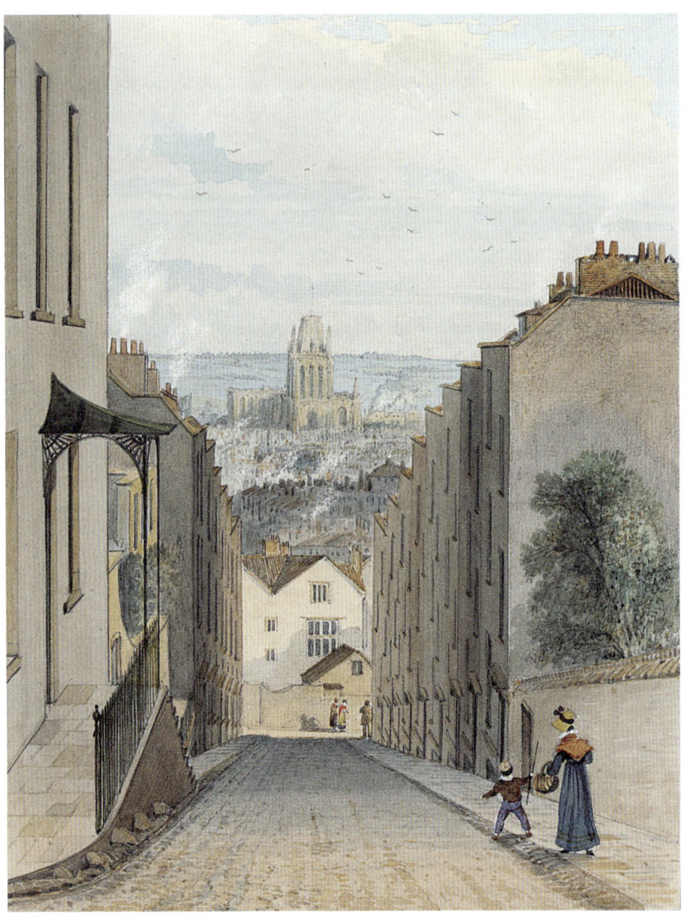

64 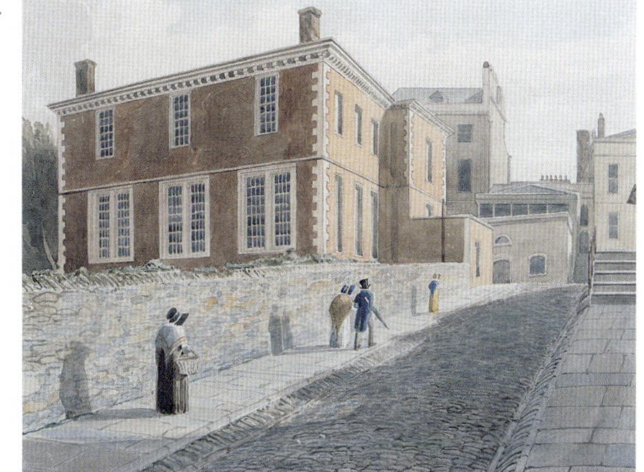

***The Red Lodge from Lodge Street* 1824**

Samuel Jackson

The Red Lodge was built on a very steep slope and in this view the ground floor is obscured by the high garden wall. The building is now a branch of Bristol Museums & Art Gallery and an Elizabethan-style knot garden has been recreated on the other side of this wall. Behind the first-floor windows are the original Elizabethan rooms which include the magnificent Great Oak Room with its ornate woodcarving, stone chimney-piece and plaster ceiling. It is a remarkable survival, given the depredations Bristol's early architecture has suffered, and it is now seen as one of the finest rooms of the period. In the early eighteenth century the house was modernised by replacing the original gables with a flat cornice and inserting the tall sash windows seen here.

At the time this watercolour was made the Red Lodge was occupied by a young ladies' boarding school run by the Misses Twigg and Kift. It later became Mary Carpenter's famous reformatory for girls. The crisis point for the survival of the house came when it was put up for sale after the First World War. Demolition of old buildings had continued and their panelling and other decorative features were often stripped and sold to those who appreciated them, often in the USA. Fortunately, a group of Bristol citizens was alerted and quickly organised an appeal to purchase the Red Lodge, which they then presented to the City.

65 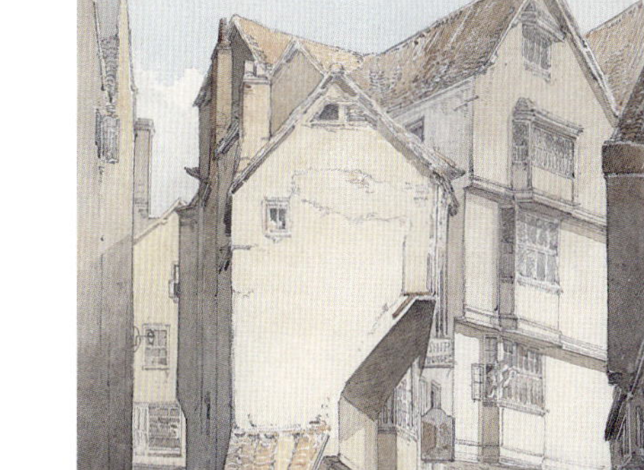

***Steep Street* 1822**

James Johnson

At one time the Welsh mail had struggled up and down Steep Street. It then had to negotiate St Michael's Hill on its way to the Severn crossings. The prominent shadow in the centre of this drawing is where a jettied house has been cut back, probably to help the traffic pass. The sign of the Ship is on the corner, a public house kept by Harry Burgess. It was a common name for a pub in Bristol.

In the summer of 1871 this very old street would be swept away by the Streets Improvement Committee. Colston Street replaced it and gave an easier gradient to Upper Maudlin Street.

66 ***The City School (Queen Elizabeth's Hospital) in Christmas Street* 1820**

Hugh O'Neill

These buildings are virtually the same today. They are at the bottom of Christmas Steps (omitted by the artist, but to the left) and the shop is a well-known fish and chip shop. In 1820 it was a broker's shop, selling second-hand furniture and household utensils.

The entrance to the charity school, Queen Elizabeth's Hospital, was through the thirteenth-century arch, originally part of St Bartholomew's Hospital. The boys were given vocational training rather than classical, and left at the age of fourteen. QEH School moved to its current premises on Brandon Hill in 1847.

More timber-framed houses at the bottom of Christmas Steps and in Narrow Lewin's Mead survived until 1969-70 when they were removed to widen the inner circuit road.

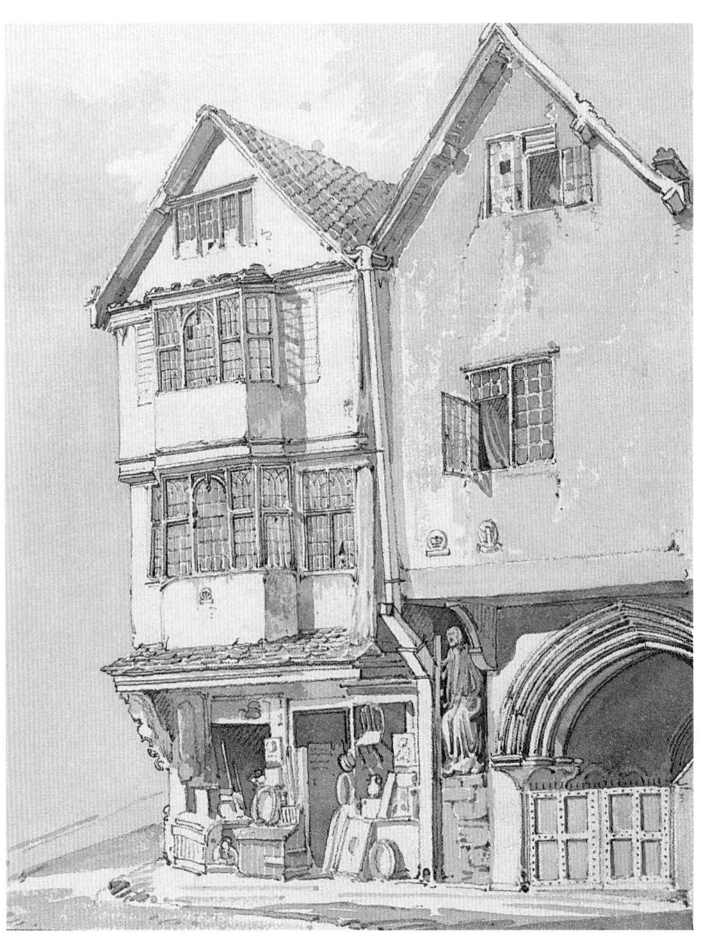

67 ***The White Lodge, seen from the garden of the City School (Queen Elizabeth's Hospital) at the St Bartholomew's in Christmas Street* 1824**

James Johnson

The White Lodge is the gabled sixteenth-century house at the top; its small tower had only recently been embellished with crenellations in the Gothic taste. The building stood opposite the King David Inn at the bottom of St Michael's Hill and although it has been said to be associated with the Red Lodge, there is no evidence. Braikenridge's interest in it was its association with the Civil War and Royalty: 'In this house prince Rupert is said to have lodged whilst in possession of Bristol'. It was demolished in the 1860s when lower St Michael's Hill was removed for the construction of Perry Road.

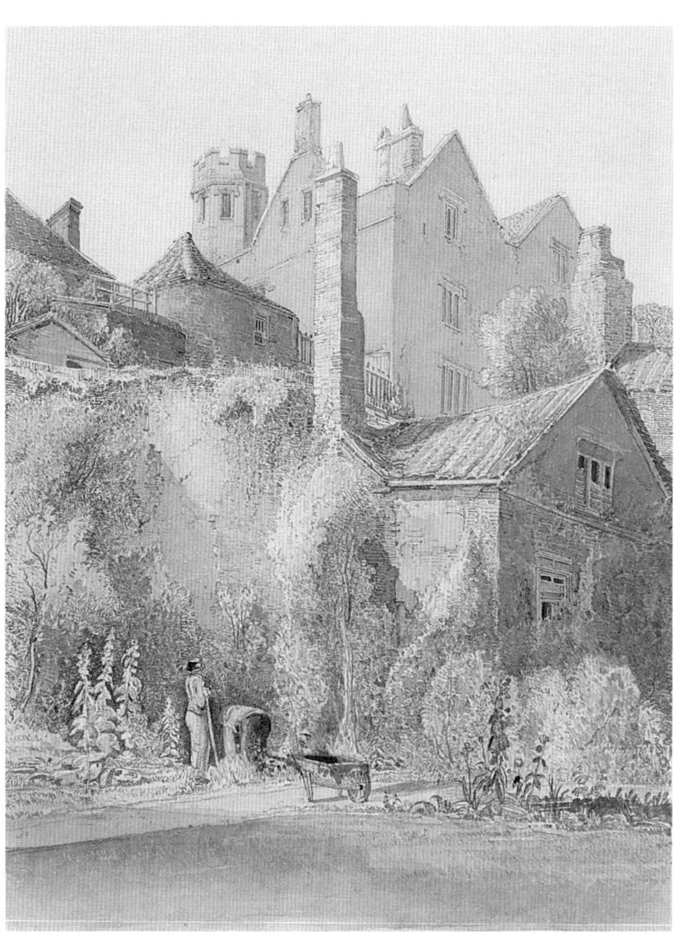

The garden of the school also served as its playground and must have been a precious patch of ground in this part of Bristol. Verbascum appears to be growing to the left of the inactive gardener. The tall chimney in the centre of the drawing gave an extra draught for fires in a house that was built into the side of a steep hill.

68 ***Queen Street (later Christmas Steps)* 1825**

George W Delamotte

Queen Street or Queen Street Steps was the original name for Christmas Steps. The steps had been installed in 1669; previous to that it had been a very steep path. The name of Christmas Steps was not in common use until after the middle of the nineteenth century.

The artist's viewpoint was from the junction of Steep Street (which drops to the right) and St Michael's Hill. The church spire is St John-on-the-Wall and behind is the tower of St Peter's.

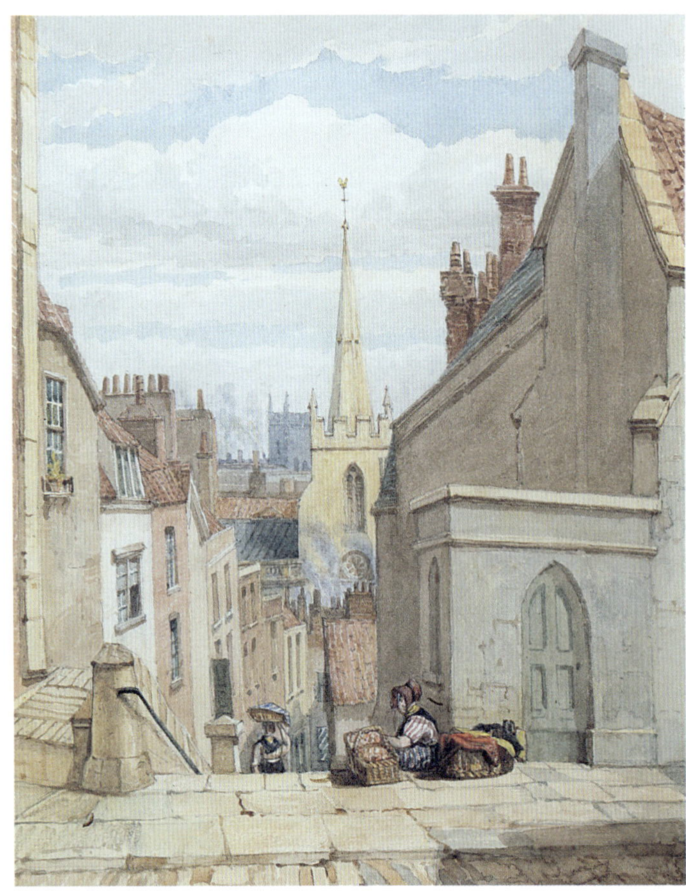

69 ***Lower Maudlin Lane* 1826**

Thomas L Rowbotham

This view looks up today's Lower Maudlin Street towards Kingsdown, with a wing of the Infirmary (now called the Old Building) to the right. The watercolour shows the original colour of the hospital which is mentioned in Latimer's *Annals of Bristol*. He wrote: 'For some inscrutable reason, the whole of the Infirmary buildings were painted black, and presented a most lugubrious appearance.' They were repainted in the middle of the nineteenth century.

The buildings with the light grey façades in the centre of the drawing are on the site of the main complex of the modern Bristol Royal Infirmary. The Blind Asylum on the left is where the blind were taught a trade; it was supported by public donations. Baskets were the principal product and could always be purchased there.

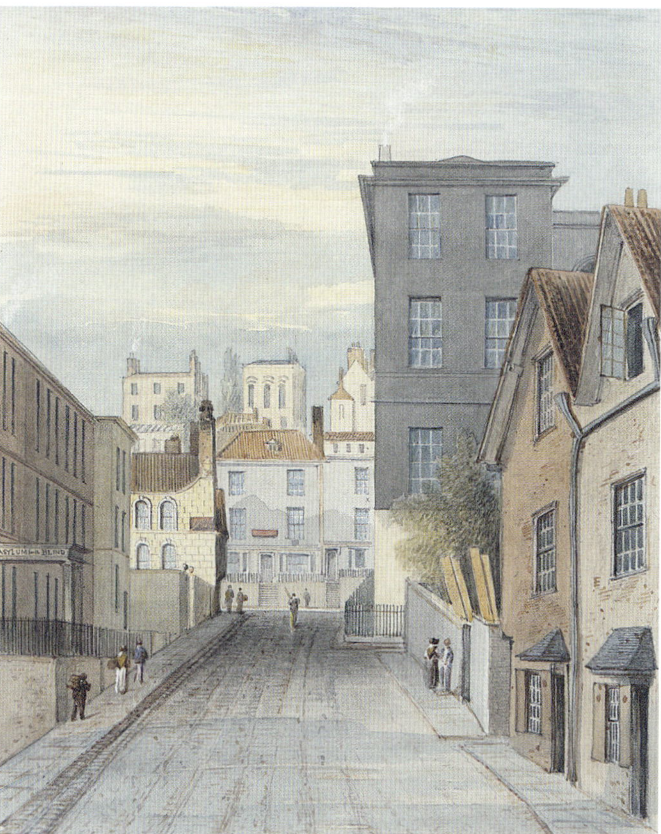

70 ***Montage Street and houses on Kingsdown* 1826**

Thomas L Rowbotham

The viewpoint is from today's bus station, with Earl Street running off to the left in the foreground and Montague Street climbing to upper Kingsdown. The woman wearing a red shawl has crossed Dighton Street and walks up what is now Montague Hill South.

The terraced houses show the variety of colour that was used for rendered Georgian façades. The pigment was probably derived from locally quarried ochre which, depending on its source, varied from light yellow to rich brown.

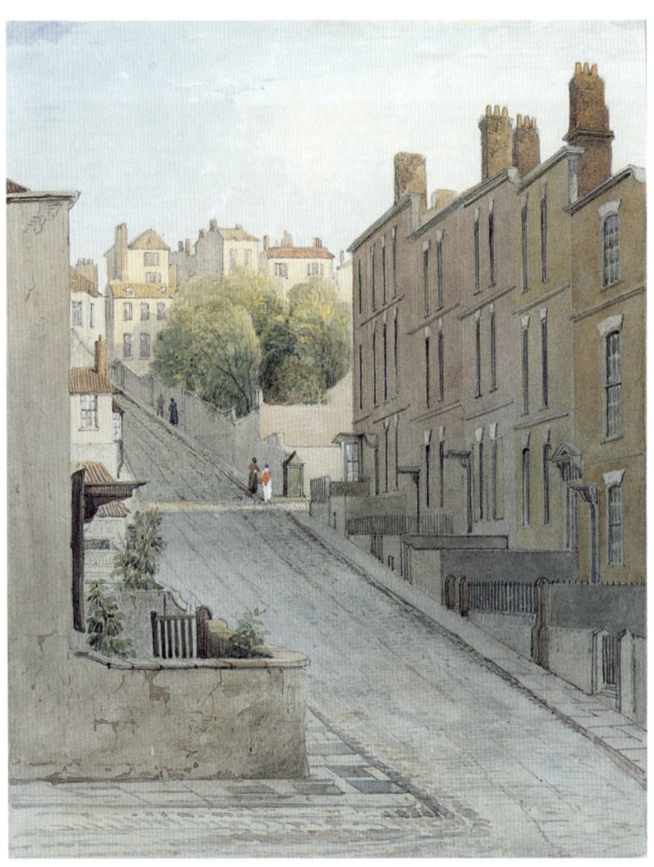

71 *Spring Hill from King Square* 1828

Thomas L Rowbotham

Spring Hill ascends Kingsdown from King Square and the upper section remains as in this drawing, including the street lamp. Its name probably derives from the springs in the area. Dove Street is the patch of light above the steps.

King Square was named in honour of George II and, although building started in 1741, the square was not completed for over twenty years. The houses on the slopes were built in the late 1750s and 1760s. Most were speculative building and sold by their builders in an unfinished state to be decorated by the new owners.

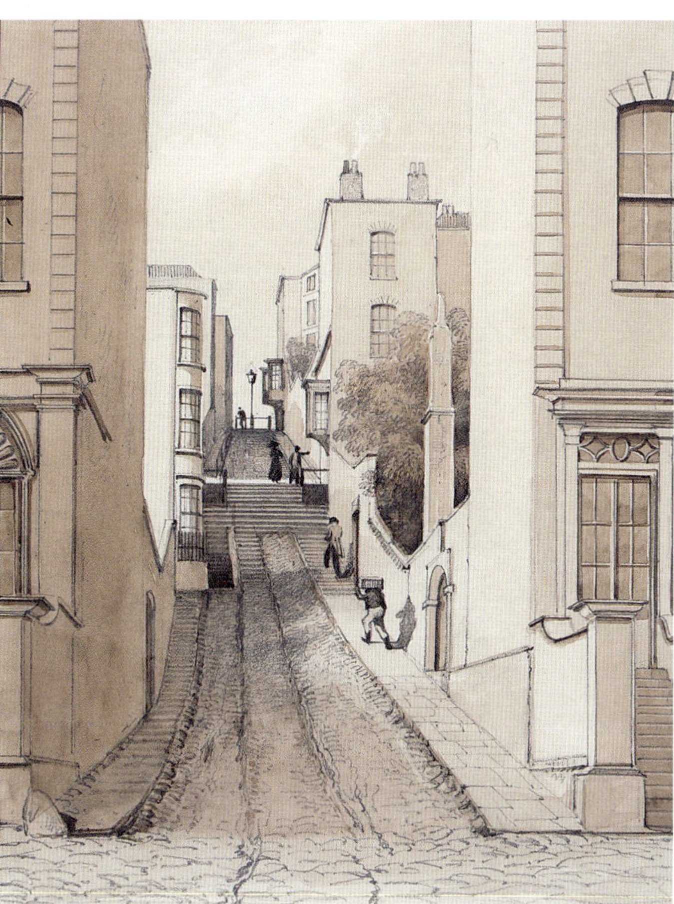

The original Kingsdown, that is on the slopes of the hill as well as on the top, was a large area laid out in the eighteenth century. It stretched from St Michael's Hill to King Square. Little was destroyed during the Blitz but large areas were razed later, despite increasing opposition, and fourteen-storey flats went up in Dove Street. Kingsdown has been described as Bristol's most important Georgian suburb and the destruction of its lower flanks in the 1960s 'was perhaps the worst of all the crimes committed in Bristol in the name of progress since the war' (Gordon Priest and Pamela Cobb (eds), *The Fight for Bristol*, 1980).

FROM BALDWIN STREET TO PRINCE STREET BRIDGE

72 ***A house behind Baldwin Street* 1823**

Hugh O'Neill

At the time of this drawing the cone in the background was used for the burning of faulty tobacco at the Tobacco Warehouse in Back Street. However, the cone must have originally been an eighteenth-century pottery or glass kiln from an as yet unidentified manufacturer's site. It is clearly shown on a map of 1742.

O'Neill made the drawing to record a house which was being pulled down. The house was surrounded by other buildings and would have been reached by an alley or yard off Baldwin Street. Living in the centre of Bristol was cramped and uncomfortable, hence the move of the prosperous to the Georgian outskirts.

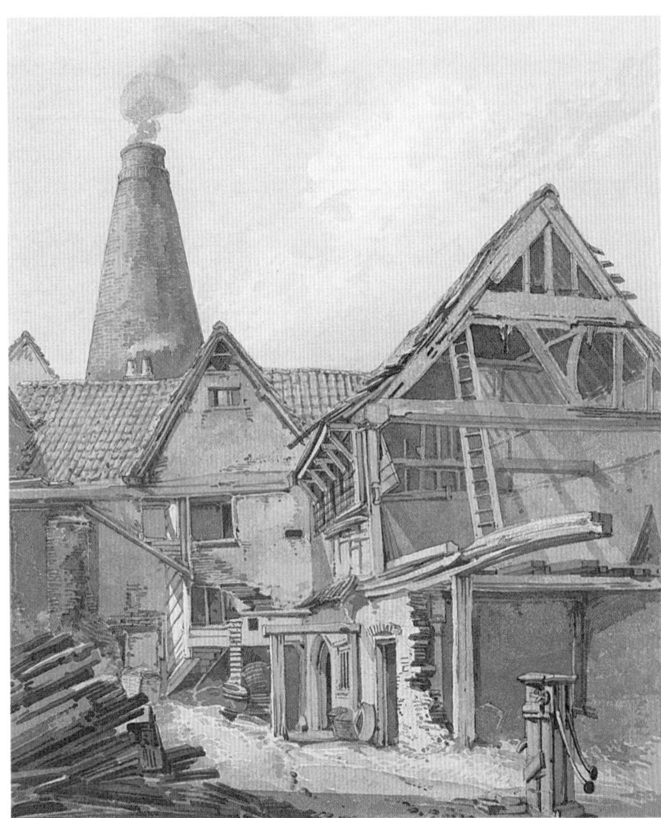

73 ***Baldwin Street* 1824**

George W Delamotte

Baldwin Street was shorter and narrower than it is today and the bend seen here is its junction with today's St Stephen's Street. In 1874 the city surveyor proposed a new thoroughfare to ease the traffic congestion in Clare Street and Corn Street. Baldwin Street was then extended by cutting through the buildings seen here on the left and continuing until Broad Quay (now the City Centre) was reached. This new Baldwin Street did not open until 1881.

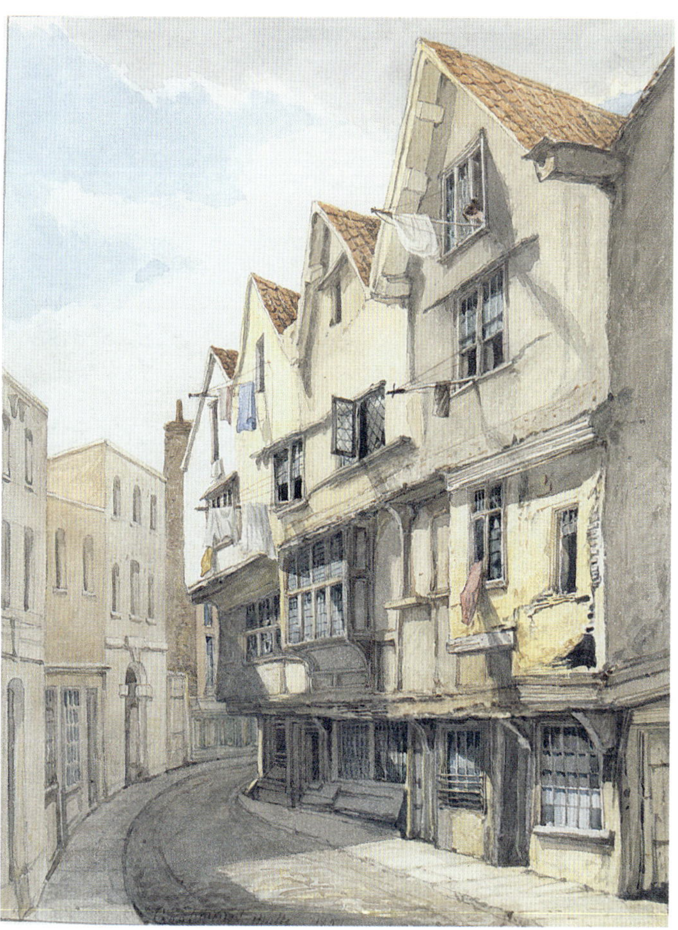

74 ***Houses on Bristol Back near the end of King Street* 1823**

Hugh O'Neill

The gabled houses on the shady side of King Street are two of the five which included the Llandoger Trow. This end was destroyed in the Blitz of 1940. Braikenridge's notes point out the White Hart public house, built against the end wall, 'much frequented by the Welsh who come up by the traders & many of whom keep the Market erected for the Welsh and called the Goose Market'. In the centre of the drawing, a seventeenth-century house has been modernised with a Georgian bow front. At this date it was a tea and china warehouse, run by Thomas Pole junior.

Cranes were an important feature of the docksides. They are shown individually on Plumley and Ashmead's map of the city and this was one of a pair on The Back. All were small and hand-operated.

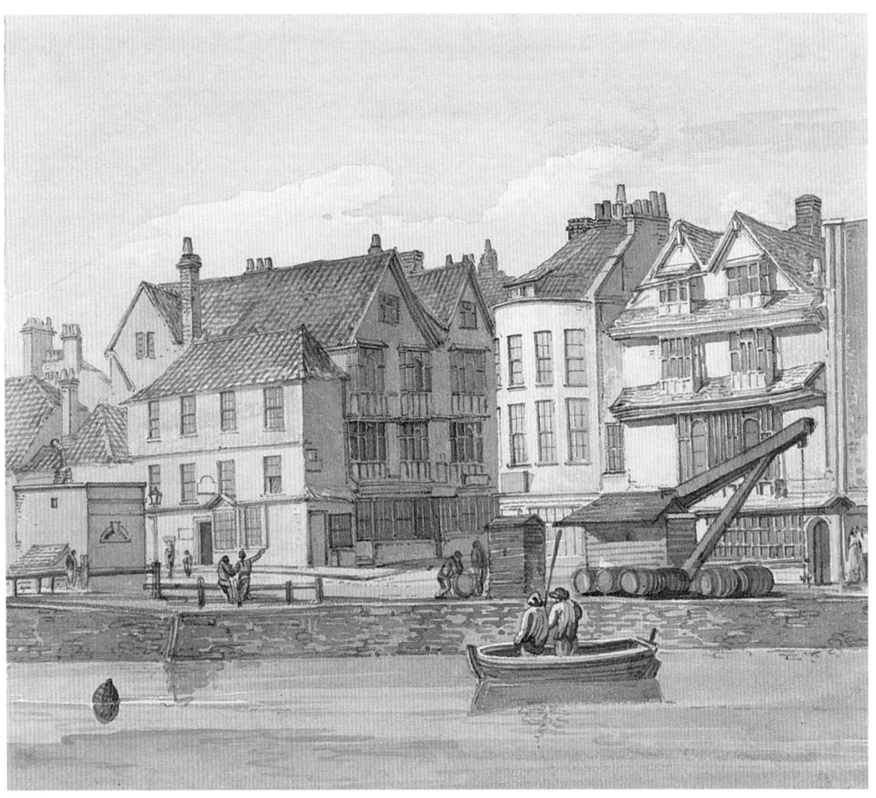

75 ***The Old Custom House on Bristol Back*** **1825**

Thomas L Rowbotham

At the time of this drawing the Old Custom House (the tallest building in this drawing, with the Royal coat-of-arms) was the Three Cups public house. It had been built in 1666 but by 1710 larger and grander premises were required and another was built in Queen Square. Bristol Back was also known as The Back and ultimately became Welsh Back.

The archway in the low wall to the right gave access to the burial ground belonging to St Nicholas' Church. On the quayside is the Welsh Market, also known as the Goose Market, where on Wednesdays pigs, poultry, fruit and nuts could be purchased according to the season.

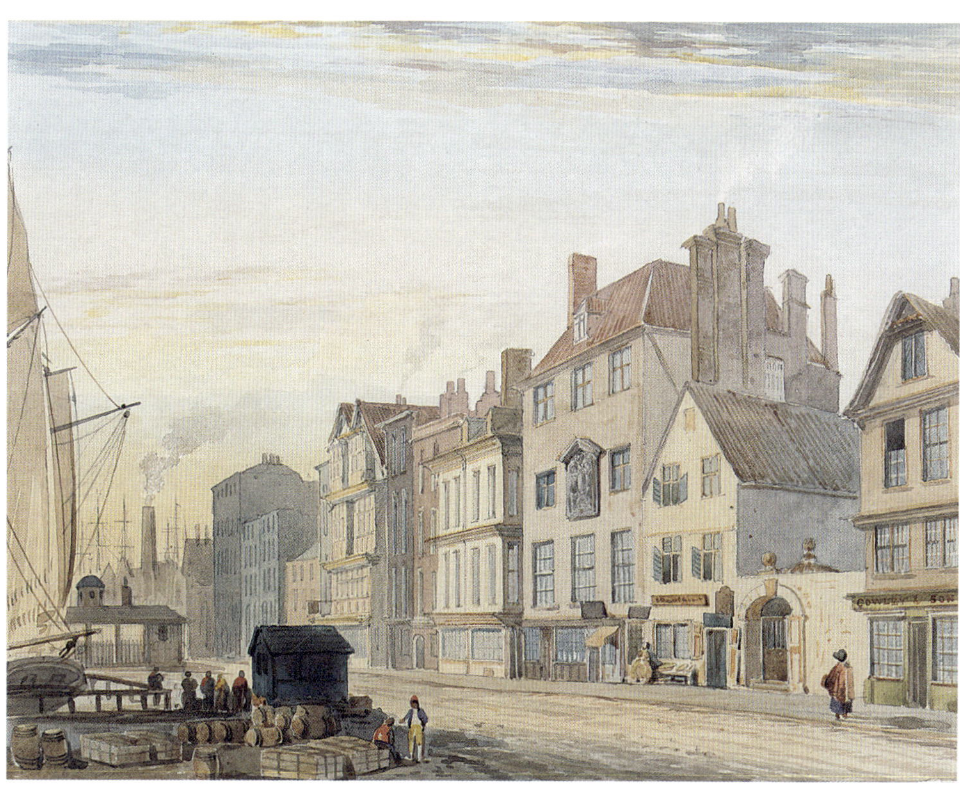

76 ***The Rackhay, off Back Street* 1821**

Hugh O'Neill

This short street has changed beyond recognition but, as in 1821, it still gives access to the back entrance or stage door of the Theatre Royal from Back Street (now called Queen Charlotte Street). However, it is now all 1960s brutalist architecture. Since the 1980s, some of the ugliest of the post-war offices have been refurbished or even replaced and a new office was designed for the corner of the Rackhay. Unfortunately it was not built.

The origin of the name Rackhay is not fully understood although the 'rack' would have been the drying racks used in the medieval woollen industry. It has recently been thought that 'hay' could come from 'hythe', meaning a landing-place, and may denote that the original course of the Frome flowed here. In the thirteenth century, when the great medieval harbour was constructed at St Augustine's Reach (see plate 50), the course of the Frome was changed and the exact route it formerly took to the Avon is not known.

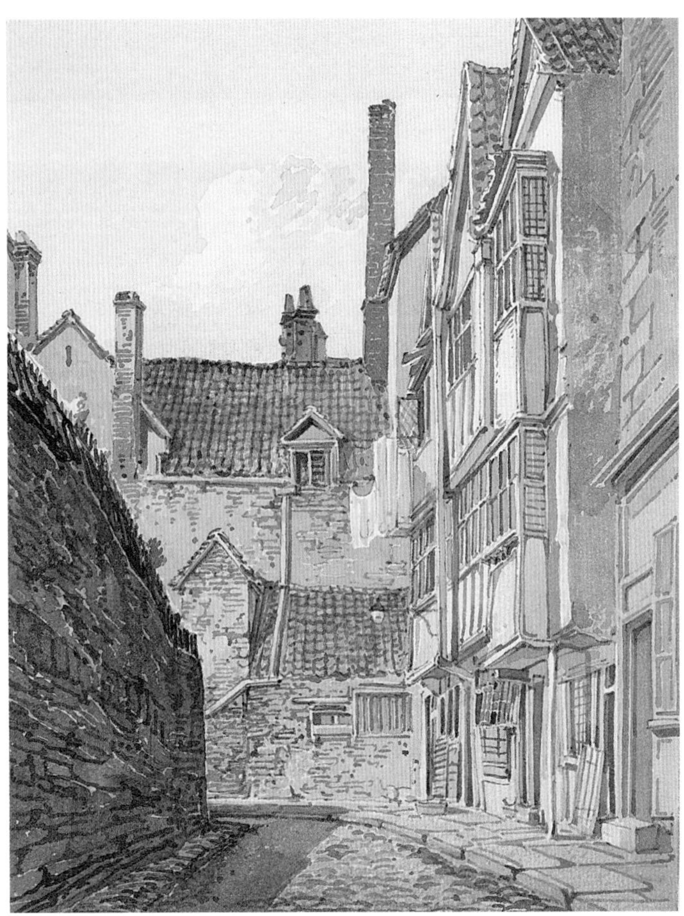

77 ***King Street* 1825**

Thomas L Rowbotham

King Street today is one of the most visually interesting of Bristol's streets with a happy mixture of buildings spanning four centuries. The signboard on the right is that of the Old Duke public house, which is still there and retains its name, although the Duke is now Ellington rather than Cumberland. Beyond are the many gables of St Nicholas' Almshouses (1652) and the grand façade of the Coopers' Hall (1744). The Hall is now the entrance for the Theatre Royal but at the time of this drawing the theatre was entered through a portico further down the street, just visible where a man stands outside it.

King Street was named in honour of the restoration of Charles II to the throne. It was laid out in 1663 in what was then a marshy area south of the former defensive medieval wall, which had run from St Augustine's Reach to The Back. An important remnant of this wall, the Marsh Wall, still remains behind St Nicholas' Almshouses. It is a bastion, which is thought to be mid-thirteenth century, and is the most substantial remains of Bristol's medieval walls which can still be seen.

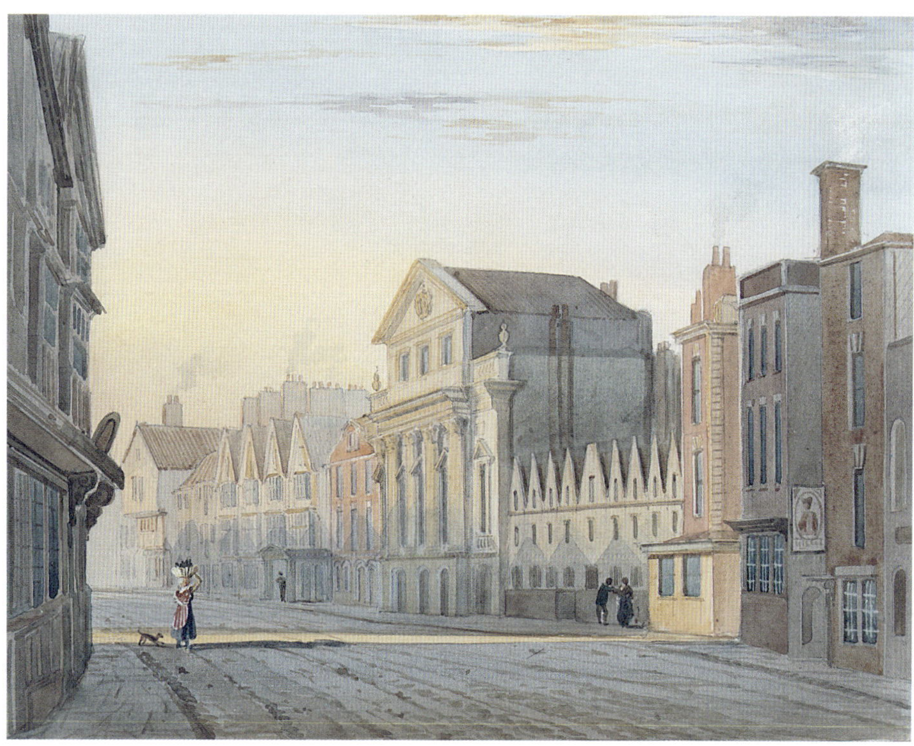

78 ***A Passage off Marsh Street* 1827**

Thomas L Rowbotham

Marsh Street (which today links the roundabout at the western end of King Street with Baldwin Street) could be reached from Broad Quay by walking through this arched passage. We are looking towards Marsh Street, which is the chink of blue light beyond the washing hung out to dry. The house above the arch was built between the backs of the houses in Marsh Street and those on the Quay, so the arch was seen only by those walking through the passage.

Bristol's older areas were characterised by alleys running between the main streets. They gave access to dark courts and the dwellings which had been squeezed into any available space. York still retains its early alleyways and gives an impression of what central Bristol was once like.

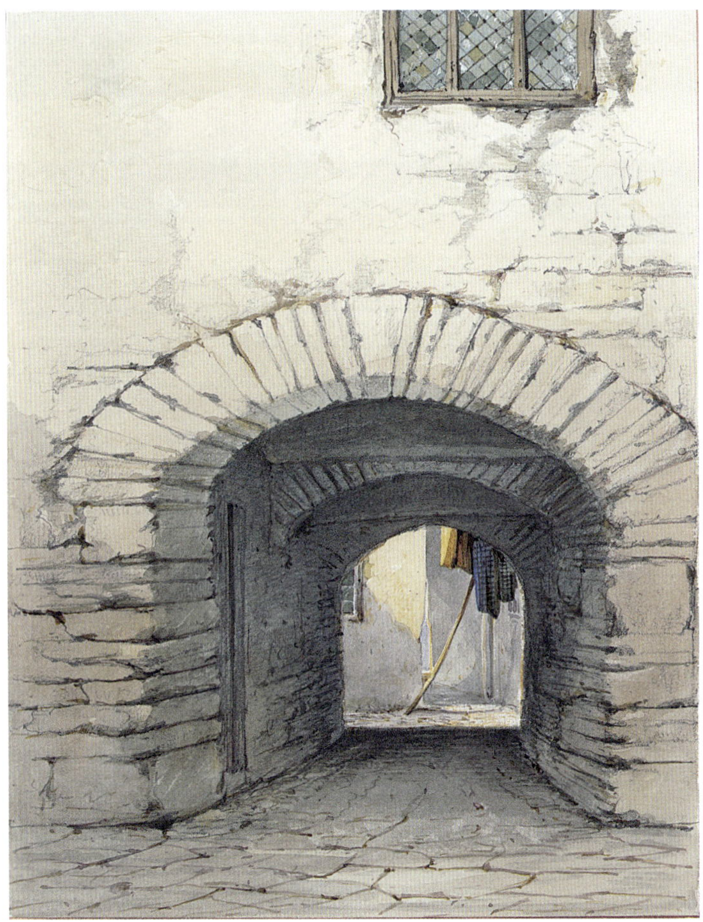

79 ***Marsh Street* 1823**

Hugh O'Neill

A sixteenth-century, or earlier, timber-framed house is being partially demolished. The chair and bed still upstairs indicates that it was not being completely knocked down.

The protrusion of older houses into the streets was regarded as an inconvenience but streets could be widened by removing the fronts of old buildings rather than by pulling them down completely. The façades were then fitted with modern sash windows. However, this house is flanked by warehouses, which may have been its fate. The tower of St Stephen's is behind.

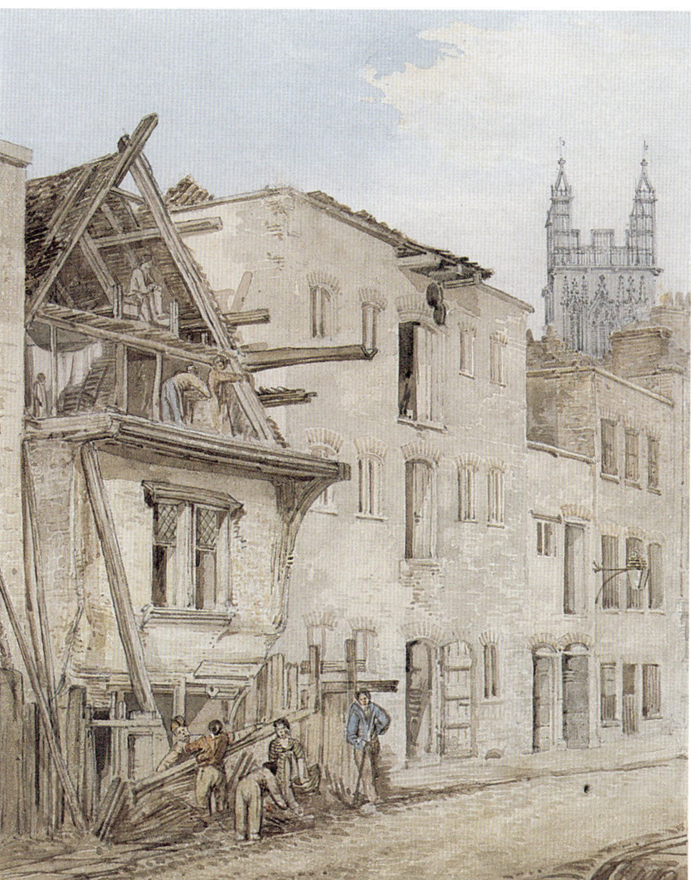

The name of Marsh Street recalls the time when the area south of the town's defensive wall was known as the Marsh. Queen Square was to be built upon it.

80 ***Prince Street 1826***

Thomas L Rowbotham

Prince Street Bridge replaced the Gibb Ferry in 1809 and a toll was levied to cross it. Its wooden structure is seen on the right of this drawing and it was swung to allow the passage of vessels. The fisherman is sitting on a long pier which extended into the harbour from the end of Prince Street.

Behind the wall on the right there was a burial ground and Braikenridge's catalogue tells us that it was used for unidentified people who had been found drowned in the harbour. It was the burial ground for St Stephen's Church and was some distance from the church. St Stephen's tower is in the centre of the drawing and the high building on the right is a sugar house.

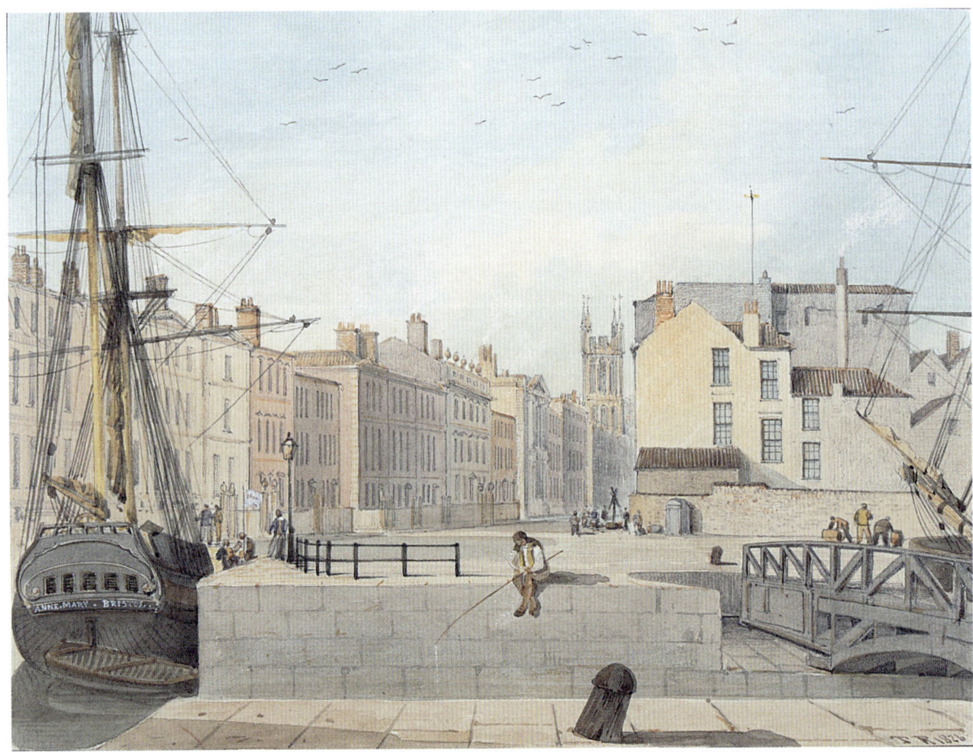

81 ***Bristol Bridge* 1823**

Hugh O'Neill

This elegant bridge is Georgian, designed by the architect James Bridges and opened in 1768, and it still survives under the wider Victorian bridge which was constructed above it. There were two toll houses on each side, by this time used as shops, and two are seen here. Behind them is the back of Bridge Street and the tower of St Mary-le-Port. High Street is on the left.

Bridges' design had replaced a traffic-congested medieval bridge with houses packed tightly along its sides, but the true appearance of this original bridge was not known until 2000. It was not until then that an historian consulting Braikenridge material in the Bristol Reference Library recognised that a mid-eighteenth century drawing there of the medieval Bristol Bridge was an authentic record (there are several spurious ones). Braikenridge's note on this small but crucial record tells us that he bought the drawing in 1803 from a bookseller who had found it between the leaves of an old book. He later placed it in one of the thirty-six portfolios of his Bristol collection, where it has been ever since. Without the diligence and care of the antiquary, and the contemporaries who knew of his interests, many details of Bristol's history and topography would have been lost.

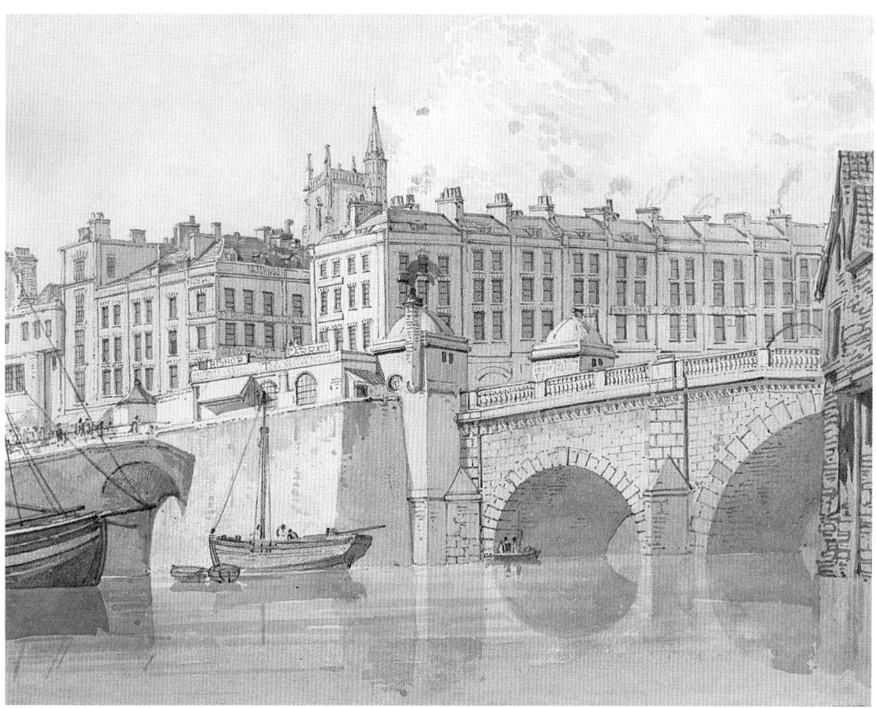

82 ***The Counterslip* 1820**

Hugh O'Neill

Counterslip today is the road joining Victoria Street with St Philip's Bridge and the name was derived from an earlier name, Countess Slip. The original street, as seen here, was slightly further north of today's street in an area that would later be occupied by the expansion of George's, later Courage's, Brewery. The right turn at the end of the street, at Uriah Glass's Coal Wharf, entered Temple Back where the ferry could be caught to St Philip's.

Braikenridge's catalogue notes are mainly concerned with the Baptist Meeting House, set back from the street behind the railings before Turner's signboard. It had opened in 1810. *Mathews' Bristol Guide* described the interior as 'neat and elegant' and 'The floor is on an inclined plane which affords all the Congregation a view of the Preacher'. William Turner, in the premises next door, was a painter, tiler and plasterer.

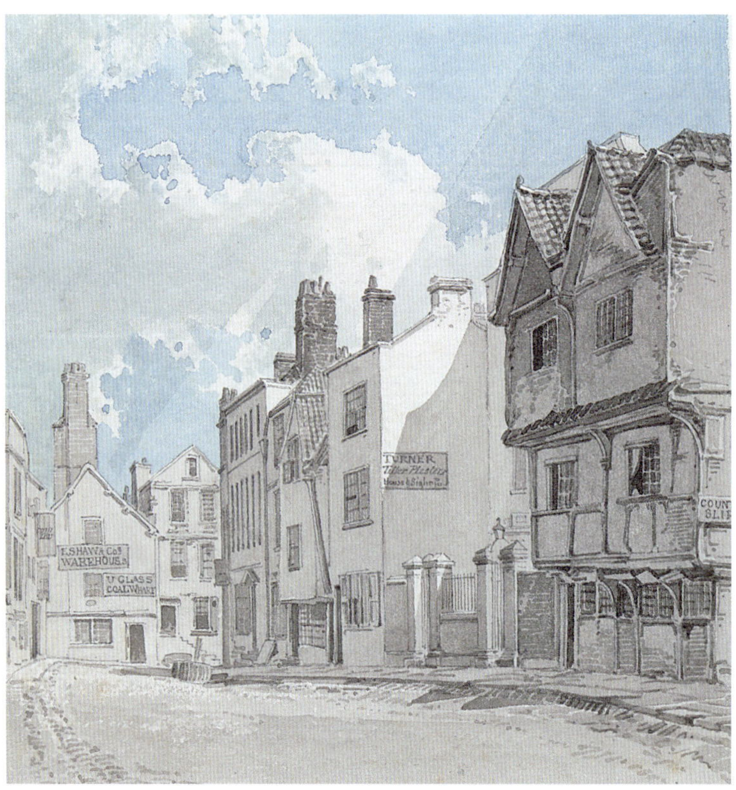

83 ***The Neptune, Church Lane, near Temple Church*** **1825**

George W Delamotte

Bristol's popular lead statue of Neptune has been moved several times during its history and has recently been re-sited in the remodelled City Centre. It was cast in 1722 by John Randall for the refurbished Temple Conduit and installed there the following year. The sculpture was originally painted and probably gilded, as it still was a century later when this drawing was made. At the end of the nineteenth century it was given a bronzed finish and in more recent years has been painted grey, both as a preservative and to resemble the lead. It would much enhance Neptune to reinstate the eighteenth-century polychrome finish.

As can be seen here, conduits were used for washing clothes and the supply of drinking water. There are several drawings in the Braikenridge Collection of women carrying pottery jars on their heads through the streets. The water for Temple Conduit was piped from springs on the Totterdown bank of the Avon; the source is in tunnels under the 'Three Lamps' signpost.

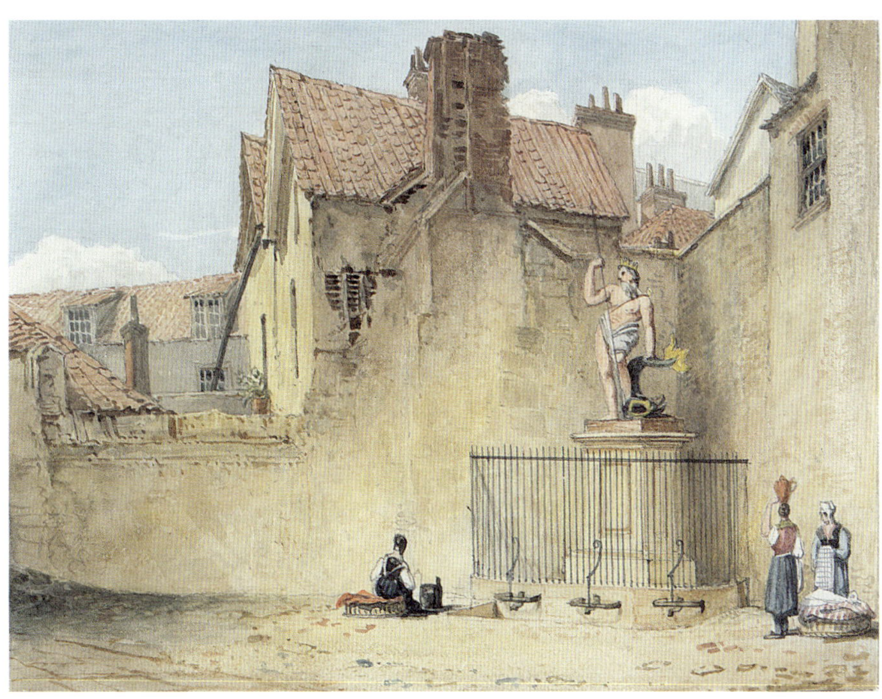

84 ***Temple Street* 1828**

Thomas L Rowbotham

This view looks towards Temple Church from the northern end of Temple Street. Travellers approaching Bristol from the Bath Road had to pass along the street to reach Bristol Bridge and Robert Southey wrote that it 'displayed as much filth, and as much poverty, as I have seen in any English town' (*Letters from England*, 1807). With the coming of the railway in the 1840s the narrow street was seen as even more inconvenient and the construction of a new thoroughfare, Victoria Street, was recommended. This did not happen until the 1870s.

The early Gothic Revival building towards the end of the street, fronted by railings, was Dr White's Almshouse. The original early-seventeenth century almshouse was replaced, or simply re-fronted, with this modern Gothic façade in 1824-5. It was perhaps designed by Hugh O'Neill as drawings by him for the façade, made in January 1824, exist in the Braikenridge Collection. As he died that April they may have been adapted by another as the completed building was slightly different.

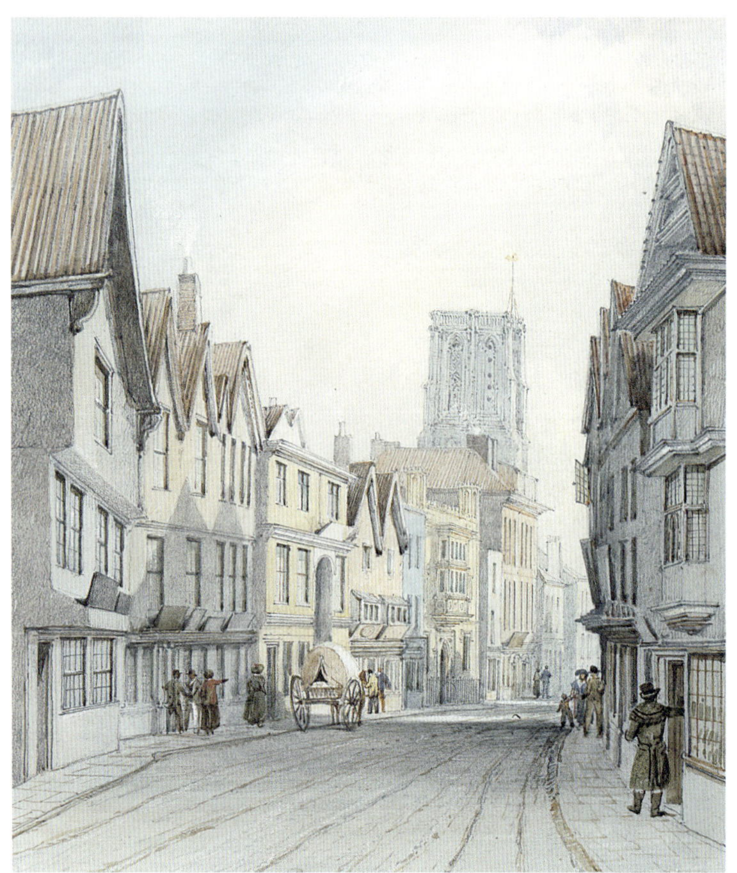

85 ***The Weavers' Chapel, Temple Church* 1828**

James Johnson

The Weavers were one of the medieval trade guilds and their chapel was in Temple Church. The fragments of stained glass which can be seen here in the east window were early-fifteenth century and included devices of relevance to the weavers' trade.

The eighteenth-century Bristol craftsman William Edney made the wrought iron gates and railings, which are seen here over a seventeenth-century wooden screen with arcading. Some ironwork was removed to the Lord Mayor's Chapel when Temple Church was gutted in the Blitz. Edney's work here and in other Bristol churches is noted for its exuberant scrollwork.

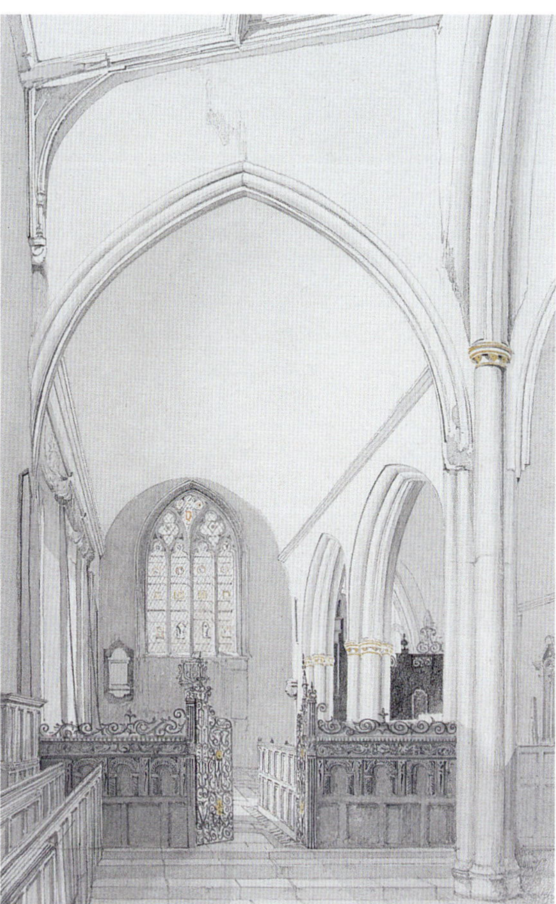

This is one of the fifteen superb architectural drawings Johnson made for Braikenridge in the summer of 1828. They show a great sensitivity for space and light as well as the glories of Gothic architecture.

86 ***Burton's Almshouses, Long Row* 1824**

Edward Cashin

Long Row ran between St Thomas' Street and Temple Street. These almshouses had been founded by Simon de Burton in 1292, an eminent citizen who had served as Mayor six times. The almshouses were rebuilt twice, this is a Georgian façade, and they were destroyed in the Blitz. At the time of this drawing they housed sixteen widows who received two shillings and sixpence per week from the parish of St Thomas plus a small donation from the Council.

The detail of the chickens running towards the cloth being shaken over the wall, in hope of crumbs, is typical of Cashin.

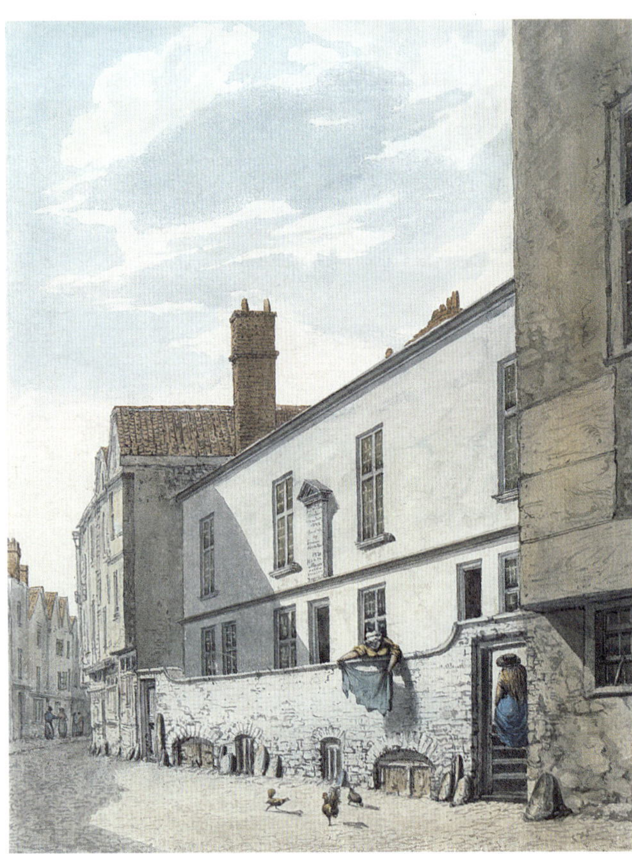

87 ***St Mary Redcliffe seen from Redcliffe Street* 1828**

Thomas L Rowbotham

Redcliffe Street was the main thoroughfare for traffic going to and from Somerset through Bedminster and was narrow, congested and dirty. The building on the extreme left, with the signboard of a mounted horseman, was the Don Cossack public house. Further along is the sign of the Angel Inn and near the church the Three Cups and Salmon. The parishes of St Mary Redcliffe, Temple and St Thomas were a densely populated area of Bristol and their many inns, taverns and boarding houses were much frequented by sailors. A network of alleys and courtyards ran between the main streets and in the mid-nineteenth century it was calculated that these three parishes had 132 dirty, overcrowded courts where families lived in cramped lodgings without drainage or adequate water supplies.

The church is without its spire; the top section had fallen in 1446 after being struck by lightning and was not to be replaced until the 1870s.

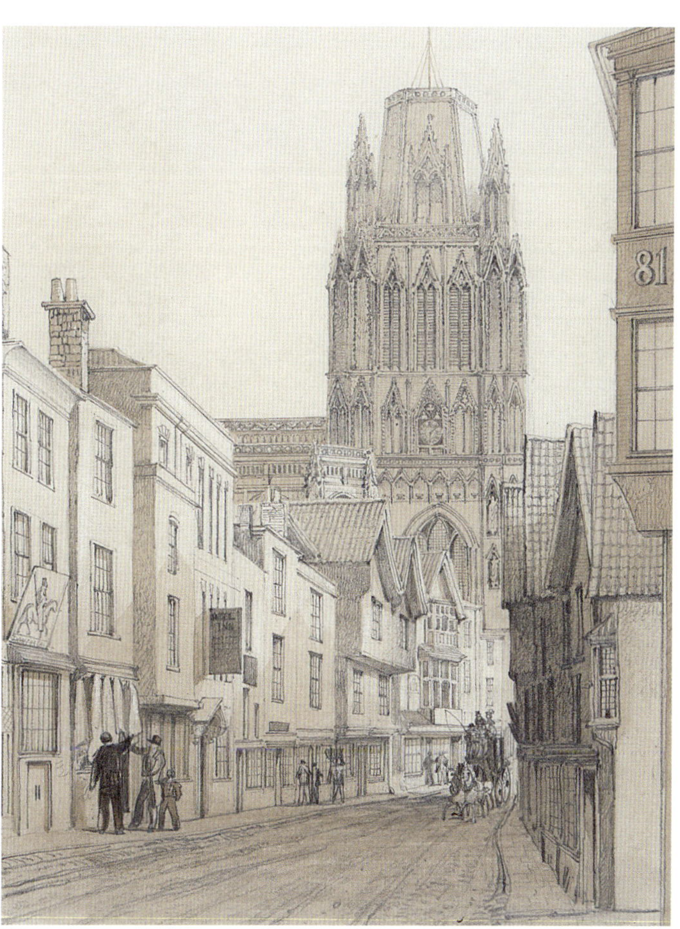

88 ***The Red Lion Inn, Redcliffe Street* 1823**

Hugh O'Neill

This drawing shows the back of the inn, looking towards its entrance from Redcliffe Street. Many of Bristol's older inns were constructed around a courtyard with open balconies giving access to the bedrooms. The yard would have accommodated all the bustle associated with the arrival and departure of stage coaches.

The Red Lion was taken down in 1864 and replaced with warehouses.

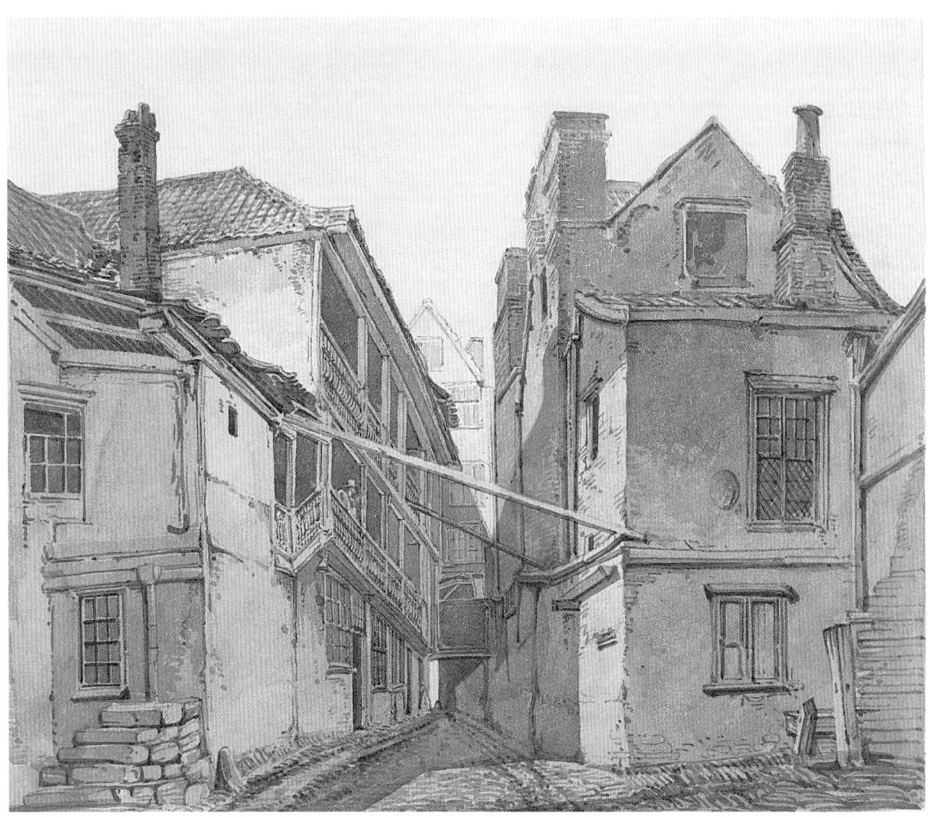

89 ***Chimney-piece at 28 Redcliffe Street* 1825**

Thomas L Rowbotham

Bristol's late-sixteenth and seventeenth-century houses, built for wealthy merchants, often contained ornate chimney-pieces. Only a few survive today, and some have been moved to other buildings, but they are well recorded in the Braikenridge Collection.

This is a mid-seventeenth century chimney-piece. The sheaf of corn grasped by the clasped hands probably represents Concord. The figure at top right is Justice, with her scales, and at top left is Prudence with a mirror and snake. Hope, with anchor and crow, is beneath Justice, Faith carries a chalice and book, and Charity is at top centre surrounded with infants.

This elaborate stone chimney-piece, together with the panelling and the plaster ceiling from the room, was presented to the Museum in 1928 by descendants of J & S Powell, cork cutters, who had used the building when this drawing was made.

90 ***St Mary Redcliffe Church from the north-east* 1826**

Thomas L Rowbotham

This unusual view of the church shows the east window blocked-up, for that was where the enormous altarpiece painted by William Hogarth stood. The triptych is now in St Nicholas' Church and is part of the Museum's collection.

Rowbotham made his drawing from some waste ground which in the previous century had been part of a garden belonging to Samuel Taylor, co-owner of the Red Lane glasshouse from the mid-1750s. Braikenridge's catalogue includes a description of the garden: 'It formerly consisted of 6 or 7 Acres of useful and ornamental Garden Ground, Shrubberies Terraces Etc extending from Temple Gate nearly to Redcliff Church & adjoined the residence of Saml. Taylor Esq. in whose Possession it was & who had so ornamented it. It contained in his time many leaden Statues with a Jet d'eau & pond for Gold & silver fish.' Taylor's 'very ancient' house was now converted into a colour manufacturers' warehouse and his garden was gone.

This drawing may show the remnant of a pool from the garden, behind the chicken on the left. Although the chickens give a rural feel, this was a heavily industrialised part of Bristol with several glasshouses still in production and other manufactories nearby. The cottages on the right are the back of Pile Street.

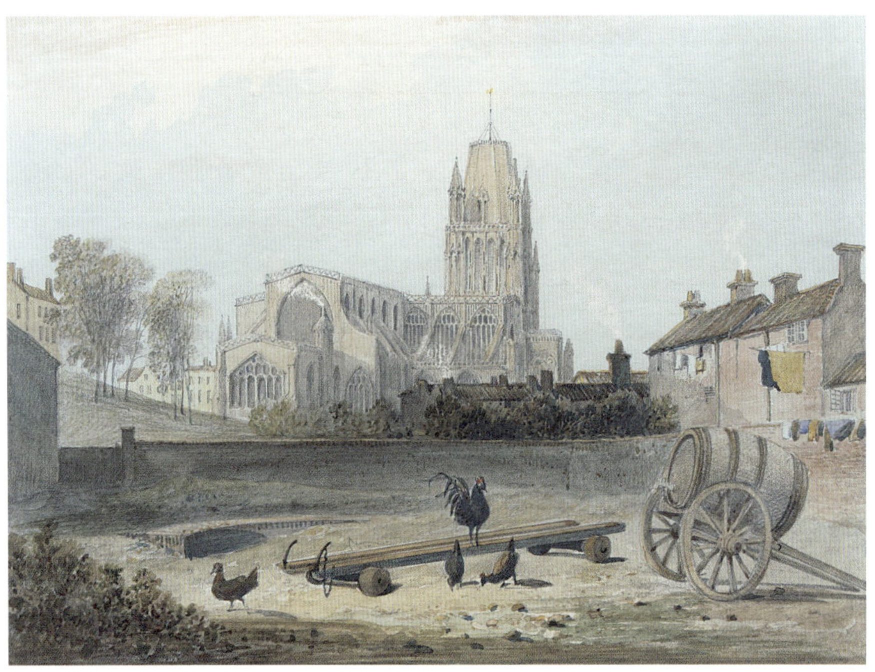

91 ***Redcliffe Hill with the Shot Tower* 1822**
Hugh O'Neill

The Shot Tower survived until the late 1960s when it was demolished during the widening of Redcliffe Hill and it is still remembered with affection by many Bristolians. Its first proprietor had been William Watts, a plumber, who in 1782 invented a new method of making lead-shot by pouring molten lead through a sieve and allowing it to fall a great height into water. He later sold his patent and turned to building speculation but went bankrupt building Windsor Terrace.

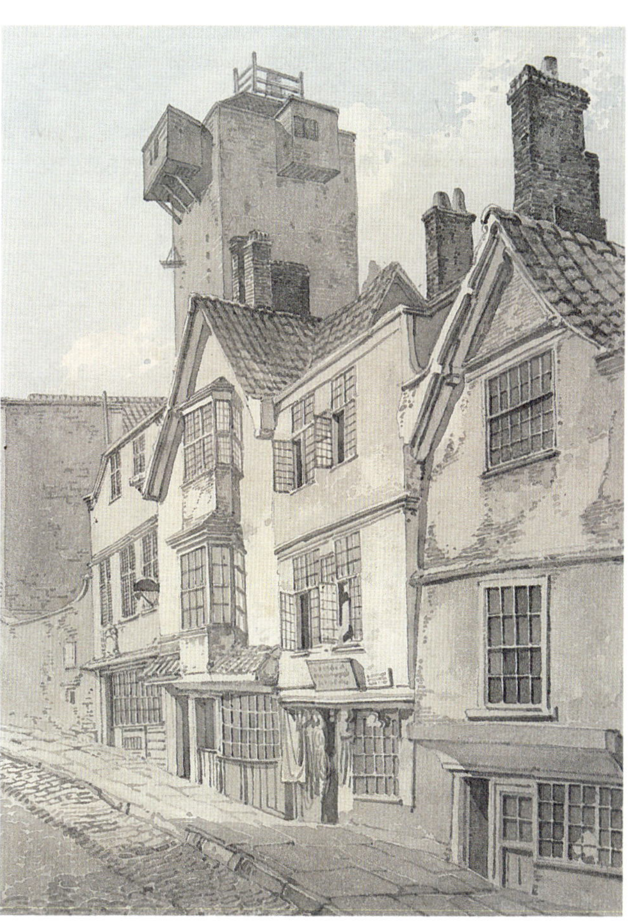

In 1968 a stylish replacement shot tower was built at Cheese Lane, near St Philip's Bridge, and has become an important element of Bristol's skyline. It no longer makes shot but, as a 'listed' building, is protected from the fate of its predecessor.

92 ***Hill's Bridge on the Bath Road* 1826**

Thomas L Rowbotham

South of the fields of Temple Meads a cast iron bridge crossed the New Cut. It was first known as Hill's Bridge and later as Bath Road Bridge. Both Hill's and Harford's (later Bedminster) Bridges were built by the Coalbrookdale Company to elegant designs. This main approach to Bristol by the Bath Road was through an area of concentrated industry. Behind the stand of trees on the left was a rope walk and to the right of the bridge was a brickyard. John Hare's Floor-cloth Manufactory, which can be seen in the panorama, plate 108, was also near here on the Temple Meads side of the river. The church towers of central Bristol are seen enveloped in smoke from the many kilns and factories at work.

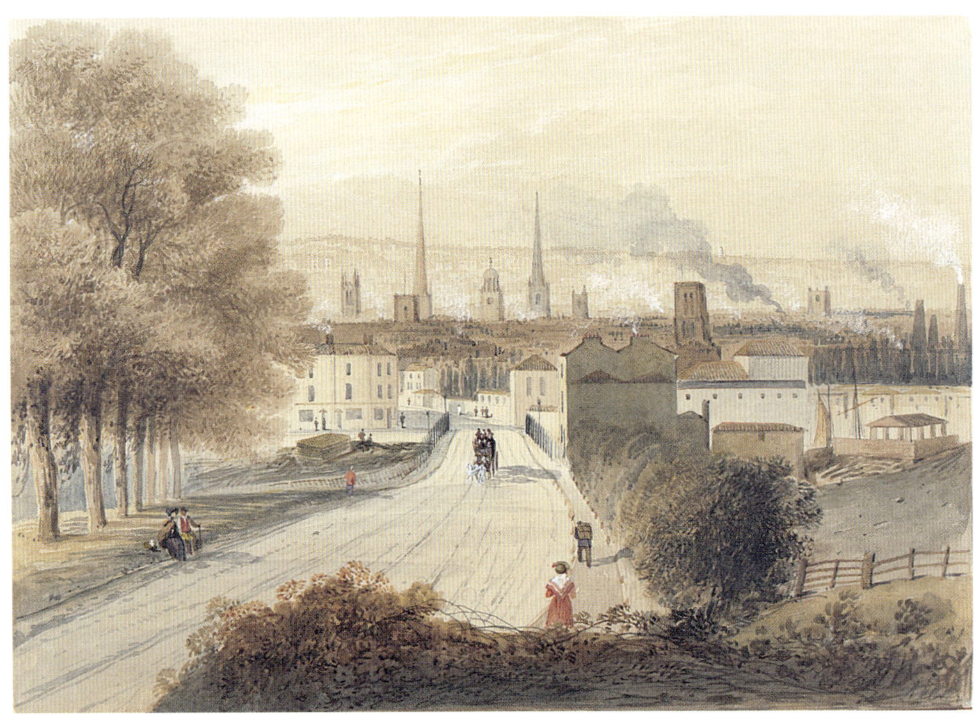

93 ***Glasshouses in St Philip's* 1821**

Hugh O'Neill

This view is especially difficult to visualise today for the artist would be standing on a platform at Temple Meads Station and looking at the office blocks along the edge of the Floating Harbour. Somerset Street, Kingsdown, is on the higher ground seen in the distance.

The glass industry was at its height in the eighteenth and early-nineteenth centuries although it survived until the 1920s. As Braikenridge wrote in 1821: 'It was formerly an observation in Bristol that the City contained as many Glass houses as Churches & the proportion of business done in this line was very great. Now the number of Glass Houses in work are reduced to a very few'. Although there were only seven firms listed in the trade directory at that date their kilns were still a major feature of Bristol's skyline.

The two kilns on the left are the Soap Boilers' glasshouse in Cheese Lane and the single kiln on the right is the Hoopers' glasshouse, Avon Street; they were named after their eighteenth-century founders. At the time of this drawing both businesses produced bottles. They were eventually to amalgamate as the same firm and, under the name of Powell and Ricketts, were the last working glasshouses in Bristol. In 1923 the company went into liquidation.

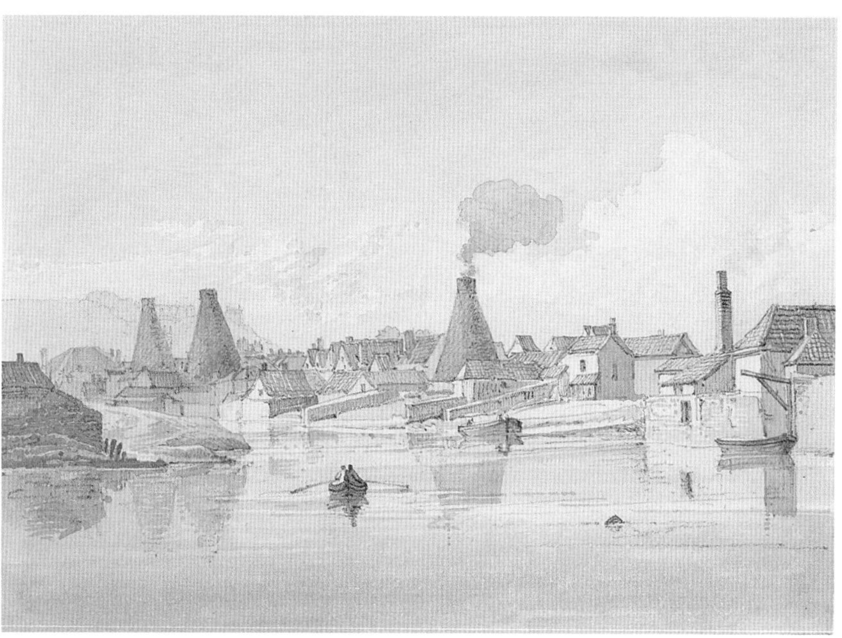

94 ***The Floating Harbour from Redcliffe Back Ferry* 1826**

Thomas L Rowbotham

Today's Redcliffe Bridge (built 1939) would be behind the viewer. The ferry seen in the foreground crossed from Redcliffe Back to Ferry Avenue (now Mill Avenue) which connected Welsh Back to Queen Square. There were three main ferries that crossed the Floating Harbour in the 1820s and they were of vital importance as the only bridges were Bristol Bridge and Prince Street Bridge. The other ferries ran from Temple Back to Passage Street (replaced by St Philip's Bridge in 1838) and Guinea Street to The Grove. The standard fare was one halfpenny.

The church towers on the skyline can still be seen from Redcliffe Bridge and have not been obscured by later buildings. They are, from left to right, All Saints', Christ Church, St Nicholas' and St Mary-le-Port. On the left, coastal traders, many probably bringing in produce for the markets, are moored on Welsh Back.

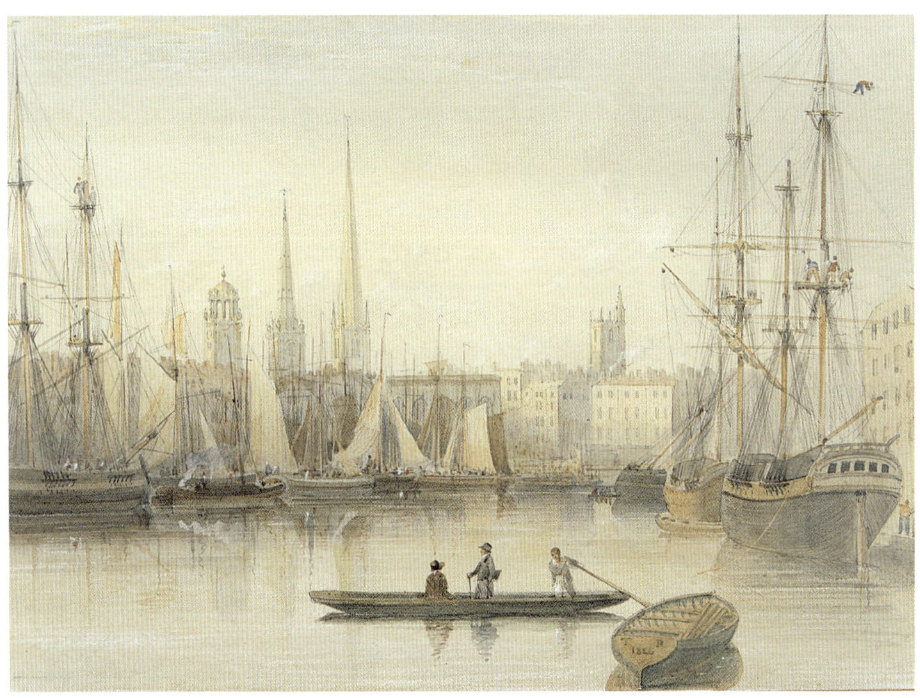

95 ***Bathurst Basin* 1825**

Edward Cashin

The Avon is tidal into the heart of Bristol and previous to the construction of the Floating Harbour the moored shipping was deposited onto mud banks at low tide. The new harbour, constructed in 1804-9, overcame this problem and provided a permanent high tide by damming the Avon, constructing locks, and digging the New Cut to carry the flow and tidal waters of the river.

Bathurst Basin was enclosed by two sets of locks and was constructed along the old course of the Malago river, which flows down to Bedminster from the flanks of Dundry and originally joined the Avon here. The Basin was built during the construction of the Floating Harbour to link the new non-tidal harbour with the tidal New Cut. It provided a second entrance to the harbour, the principal entrance being at Cumberland Basin.

Guinea Street is behind the lock and bridge and to the right the low building with the smoking chimneys is Acraman's Ironworks, where anchors, chain cable and much of the ironwork needed for shipbuilding was forged. The very large building in the centre was a former sugar house which was in use as a bonded warehouse for West Indies produce. Bristol General Hospital, built in the 1850s, now stands on this site.

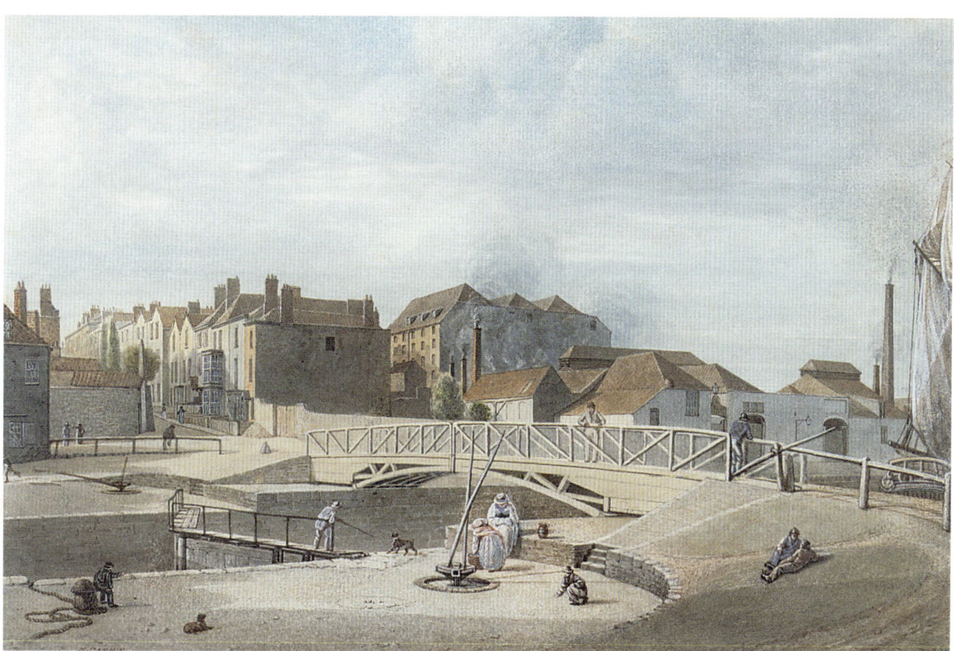

96 *Eastern Wapping Dock* 1826

Thomas L Rowbotham

Scott and Patterson's Yard was on this site, near Prince Street Bridge, which is now occupied by the housing development called Merchants' Landing. William Scott rented the yard for much of the 1820s and William Patterson was his assistant; Patterson later took over the business when Scott was bankrupted. The ship seen on the stocks to the left, nearly ready for launching, was the barque *Avon* built for the Bristol merchants Gibbs, Son & Bright for the Black River trade in Jamaica.

The smoking chimney near the centre was at Acraman's Ironworks on Bathurst Basin.

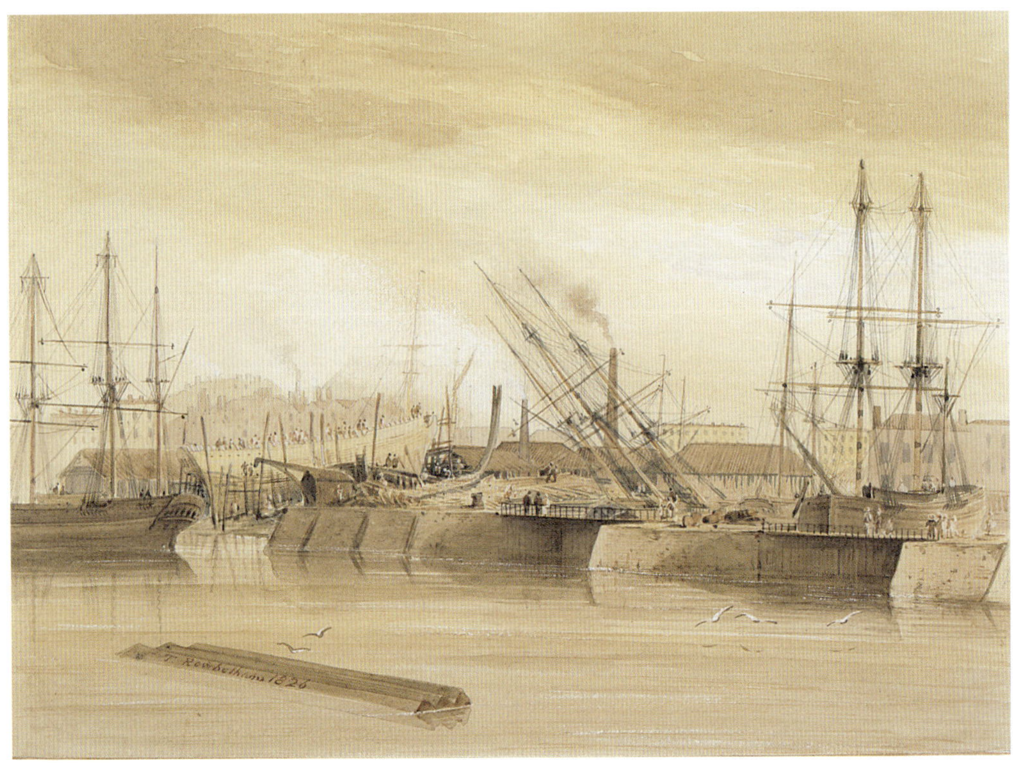

97 ***Eastern Wapping Dock with the launch of the barque* Avon 1826**

Thomas L Rowbotham

This shows the same event as the drawing opposite, but viewed from the other side. Here we look towards the Floating Harbour, near Prince Street Bridge, on the morning of 2nd March 1826. The barque *Avon*, a small vessel decorated with flags, is ready to be launched.

The function of the distinctive decorative structure has recently been debated by maritime historians. The consensus is that it is a form of viewing platform used to line-up the masts as they are stepped (fixed) and also to dock the vessels accurately. The sheer-legs on the boat on the left were a form of crane and the stepping of the masts is currently in progress.

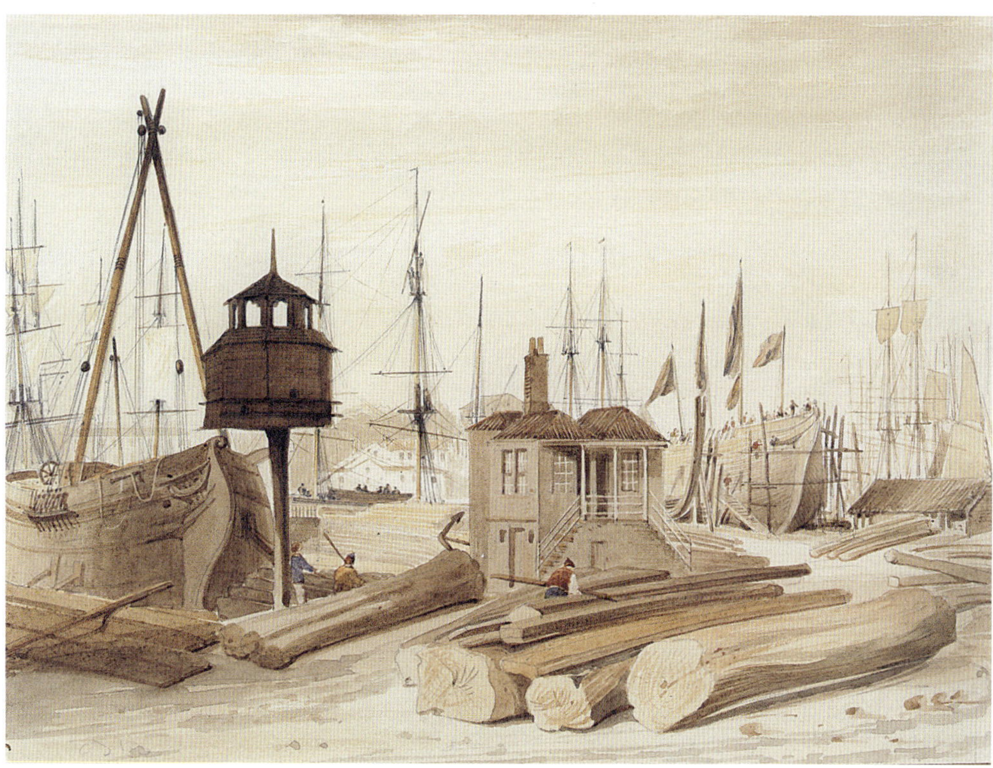

98 ***Western Wapping Dock* 1826**

Thomas L Rowbotham

This dock was on the site of today's Bristol Industrial Museum. Braikenridge's catalogue entry for the drawing is especially informative and shows his legendary attention to detail: 'the large Ship outside the Dock Gates taking in her Mizzen Mast is the Middleton of London – on the right the Vessel on the Stocks is [in] Tippetts Yard'. He also detailed the points of interest on the horizon. From left-to-right: the rotunda at Goldney House, houses nearby known as Clifton Wood, the tower of St Andrew's parish church at Clifton, and Brandon Hill with Queen's Parade beneath.

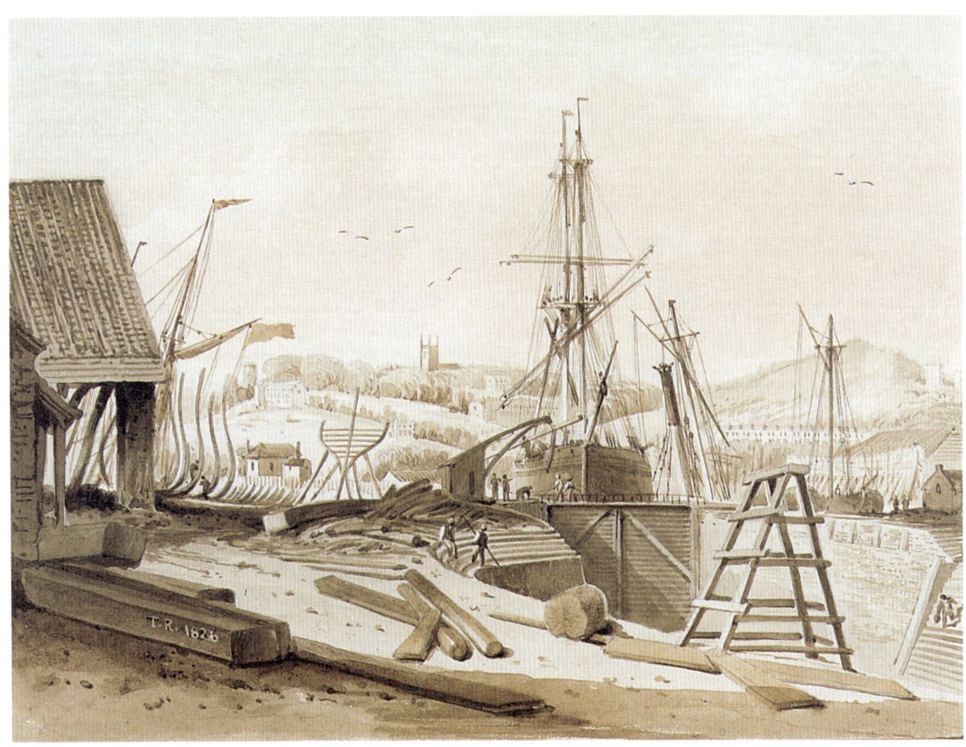

99 ***The Floating Harbour, looking towards St Mary Redcliffe and the back of the New Gaol*** 1822

Hugh O'Neill

The new prison, seen on the right, had been completed in 1820 as a replacement for Newgate prison. It had the New Cut on one side and the shipyards at Wapping on the other. Today this is the section of the harbour between the Bristol Industrial Museum and the ss *Great Britain*, along which the Harbour Railway runs.

A description of the prison in *Mathews' Bristol Guide* sounds more like an advertisement for a villa: 'this is an extensive and commodious building, which, for health, convenience, and excellent arrangement is not be be equalled in England, commanding extensive views of the surrounding country'. It was to be fired by the mob in the Riots of 1831 and partially destroyed. After rebuilding, the prison was in use until 1883 when the inmates were moved to a new building at Horfield. A fragment of its gatehouse remains, neglected, on Cumberland Road and part of the boundary wall can be seen incorporated into a building on the corner of Wapping Road.

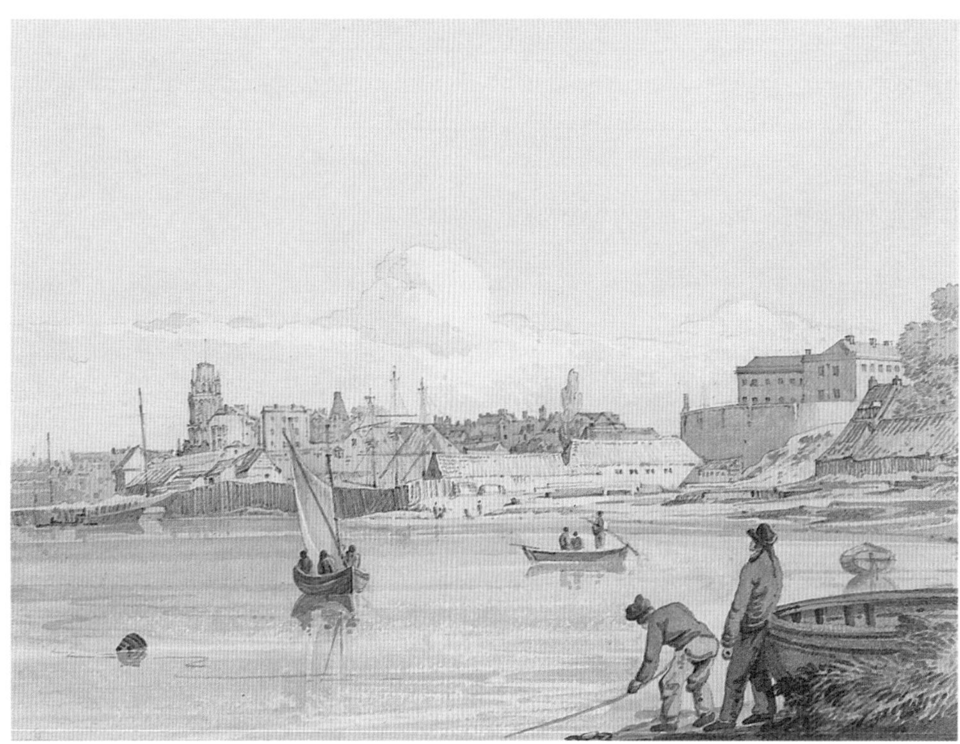

100 ***The Butts, near Tombs' Dock* 1825**

Thomas L Rowbotham

At the time of this drawing, the wooden Green's Bridge crossed the entrance to one of the small docks at Dean's Marsh, on the eastern side of Canon's Marsh. From the mid-eighteenth century it had been the dry dock run by the Tombs' family but at this time was owned by the shipbuilder John Green. However, Braikenridge wrote that it was commonly called Toms's Dock. It is possible that 'Tombs' was pronounced 'Toms' and the dock was still known by the name of its former owners.

The view looks towards today's City Centre with vessels moored on both sides of St Augustine's Reach. The tower of St Stephen's is on the right and a signal flag is flying on this bank (see plate 54). This area is now occupied by the Watershed Media Centre, and a road nearby is called The Butts.

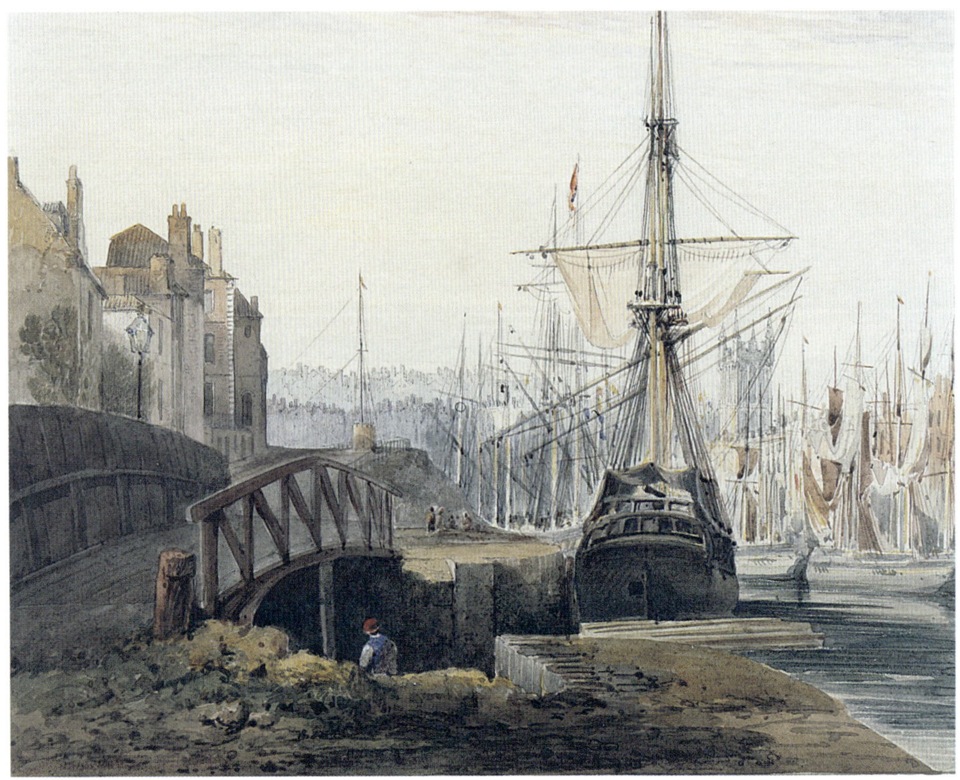

101 ***The Quay, looking north, with the Old Corn Exchange* 1825**

Thomas L Rowbotham

This view is along Narrow Quay, looking towards today's City Centre from opposite the Watershed Media Centre, with the church of St Michael's on the skyline. The forest of masts in the middle of a city captivated visitors and it was Alexander Pope in 1739 who had coined the perfect description of the hundreds of ships moored there: 'the oddest & most surprising sight imaginable ... a Long Street full of ships in the Middle & Houses on both sides looks like a Dream'. Sea-going ships, far from the sea, unloading on quays which were city thoroughfares had a unique attraction.

The Old Corn Exchange of the title is the chandler's premises on the right, with the colonnaded ground floor. It occupied the remains of a seventeenth-century corn market which had operated only briefly for the sale of imported corn in 1686-90, yet its name endured. Braikenridge's catalogue tells us that the building was nicknamed the 'Riggers' Exchange' as the riggers assembled there to gossip.

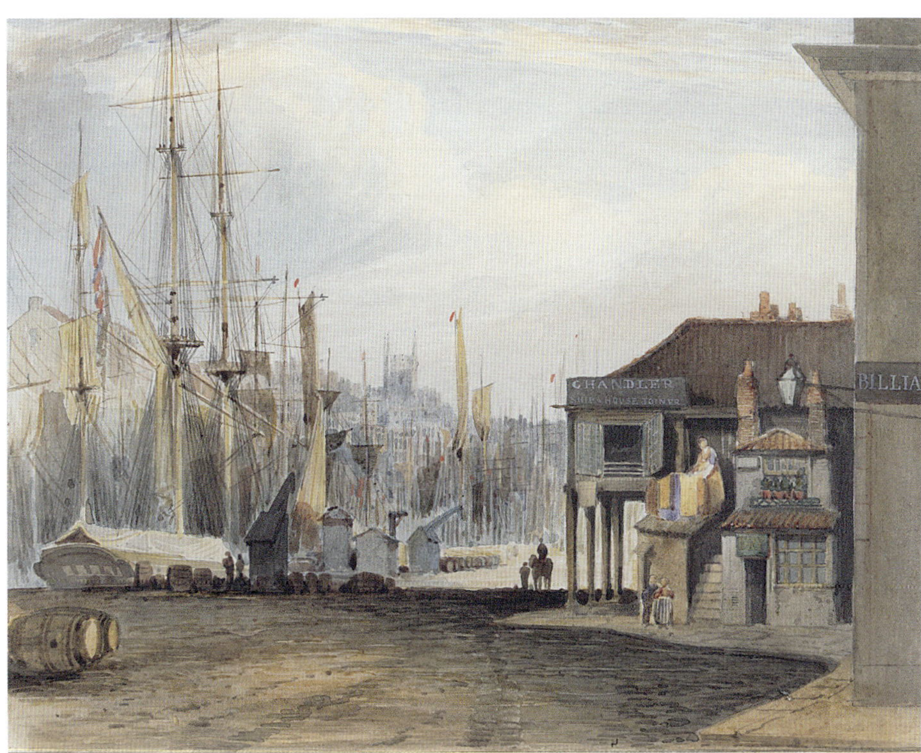

102 ***Brandon Hill and the Limekiln Dock* 1822**

Hugh O'Neill

The view is taken from near the dock where the ss *Great Britain* now lies and looks across the Floating Harbour. Brandon Hill has few trees and the Civil War fortifications are clearly seen on the top. The valley to the left is where Jacob's Wells Road now ascends. The small Limekiln Dock probably dated from the early seventeenth century; its gates can be seen on the left. It was filled-in in 1903 for the construction of the Canon's Marsh railway, a goods line. Much later, the Floating Harbour itself was under threat of being filled-in in this area. The work of the docks continued to decline and in 1969 the opportunity was seen to fill-in sections of the water to release land for office building and major circuit roads. There was a public outcry but nevertheless a Bristol City Docks Bill was passed. As it was not scheduled to take effect until 1980, and opposition continued and the property market changed, the scheme was eventually abandoned. Instead, the harbour has been successfully regenerated with the emphasis on mixed use of the area for recreation, housing and employment.

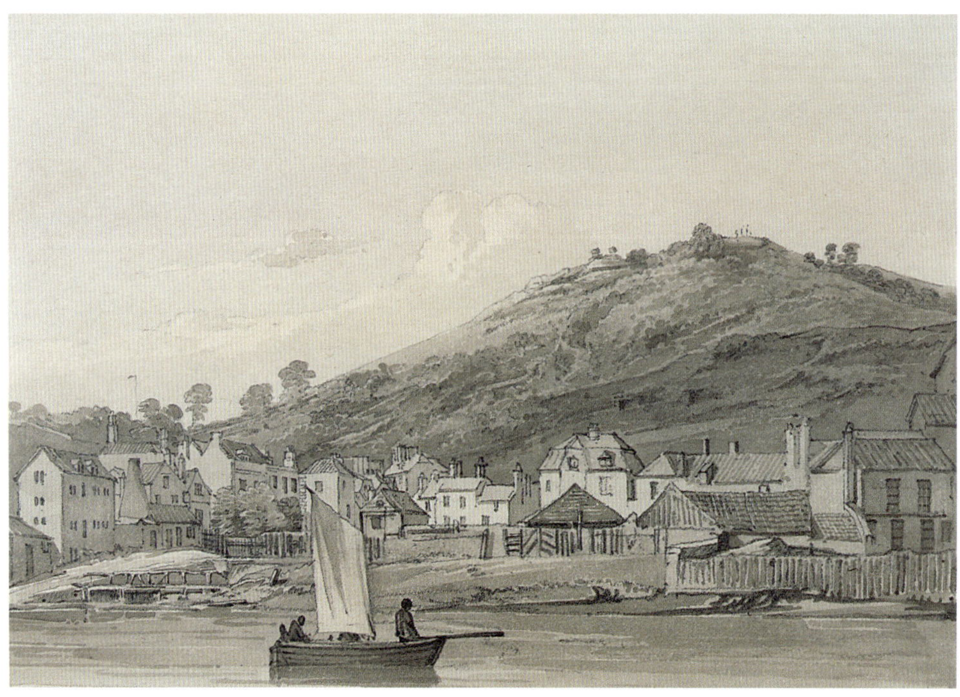

103 ***Hilhouse's New Dockyard*** **1826**

Thomas L Rowbotham

The New Dockyard, later called the Albion Dockyard, was laid out in 1820 by Hilhouse, Sons & Co. The dock is drawn from Mardyke, beneath Clifton Wood, and men are shown caulking the deck of a large East India ship. In the distance, vessels are seen in the New Cut passing Stroud's Buildings (later Ashton Terrace) a recent, rather isolated, development in Coronation Road.

From 1848 the yard was owned and operated by Charles Hill & Sons. Apart from two periods, at the beginning of the twentieth century and in the late 1970s, the yard has been in constant use, albeit no longer for the construction of large vessels. Hill's Albion shipyard closed in 1977 and a major part of the site is now a marina for leisure craft, but there is also a thriving company there which specialises in the construction of steel working boats, such as small trawlers and fishing boats.

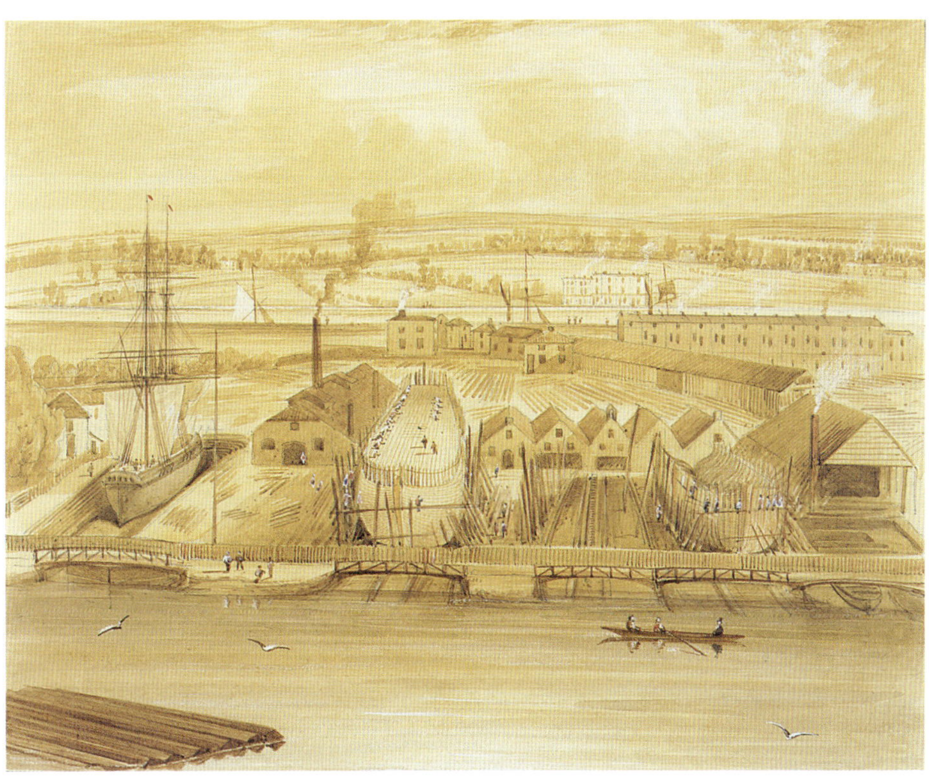

104 ***The Overfall Dam* 1827**

Thomas L Rowbotham

This view looks across the New Cut, which takes the flow of the Avon, towards Clifton, and excess water can be seen leaving the Floating Harbour at the Overfall Dam. The flow of water through the harbour was not sufficient to prevent silting and in 1832 Isambard Kingdom Brunel was consulted about the problem. Part of his solution was to change the drainage at the Overfall Dam. Four culverts were cut through the dam, with one at a deep level to take dredged mud out into the New Cut. It soon became known as the Underfall.

The small building to the right of the dam was a toll-house at the end of the Cumberland Road. The road had been a natural development of the construction of the Floating Harbour and followed the north bank of the Cut. It provided a new line of communication and visitors travelling to Clifton from Bath found it more pleasant than going across Bristol Bridge and through the city. The tolls were, of course, unpopular with local people but they endured until the early 1860s.

The Paragon is on the right skyline with Windsor Terrace below it to the left. The woods in the distance are on the Abbot's Leigh side of the Avon with Rownham Lodge on the lower hill to the left. Beneath it are Cumberland Buildings, the Dock Master's Office and the sails of ships in the Cumberland Basin.

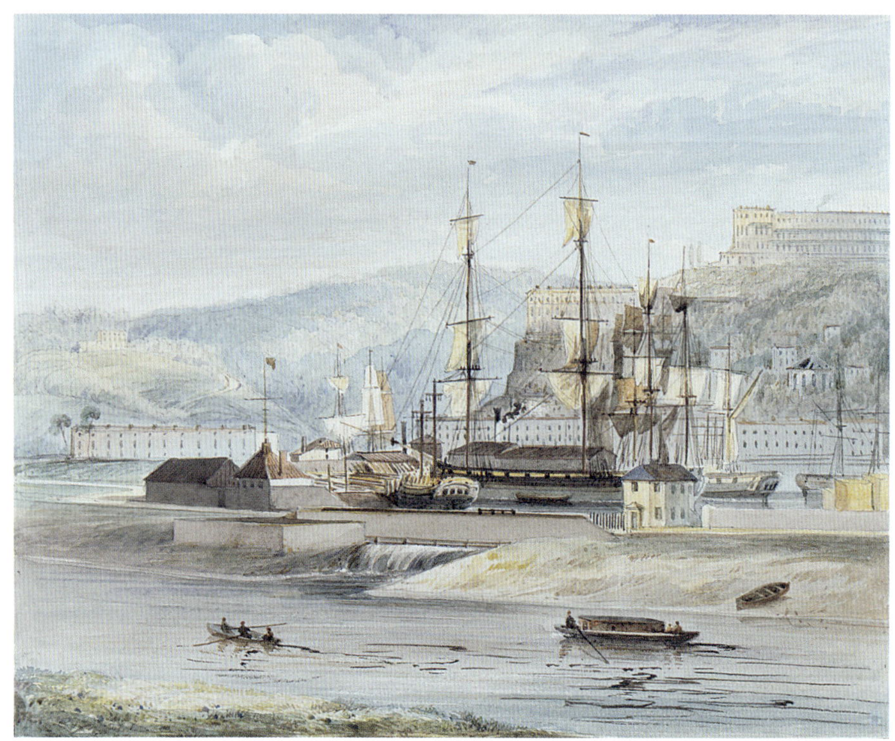

105 ***The Paragon, Windsor Terrace and St Vincent's Parade* 1823**

James Johnson

This delicate watercolour is a view of Clifton's Georgian terraces from the other side of the Avon, down-river from the Floating Harbour. Despite its idyllic appearance, all had begun as failed building speculations. St Vincent's Parade, on the river bank, had been intended as double this length. Windsor Terrace, on its massive abutment on the right, bankrupted its first developer. Most of the developments failed in 1793 and terraces remained unfinished until long after the end of the Revolutionary and Napoleonic wars. In 1824 Braikenridge wrote gloomily of Clifton '...it was little less than a bankrupt speculation to which much of the peculiar beauty of the place has been unnecessarily sacrificed.'

The avenue of trees on the bank led to the Hotwell House. Above them on the steep slope is a gazebo, probably in one of the gardens of Prince's Buildings, on the left of the skyline. The Paragon is the central, curved terrace.

It is fitting to end this small selection of drawings and watercolours from the Braikenridge Collection with the work of James Johnson. He was one of the finest watercolourists of the Bristol School of Artists and his work combines meticulous draughtsmanship with delicate washes of watercolour. His work is relatively little known outside Bristol's collection, for his career was brief and he was only 31 when he died.

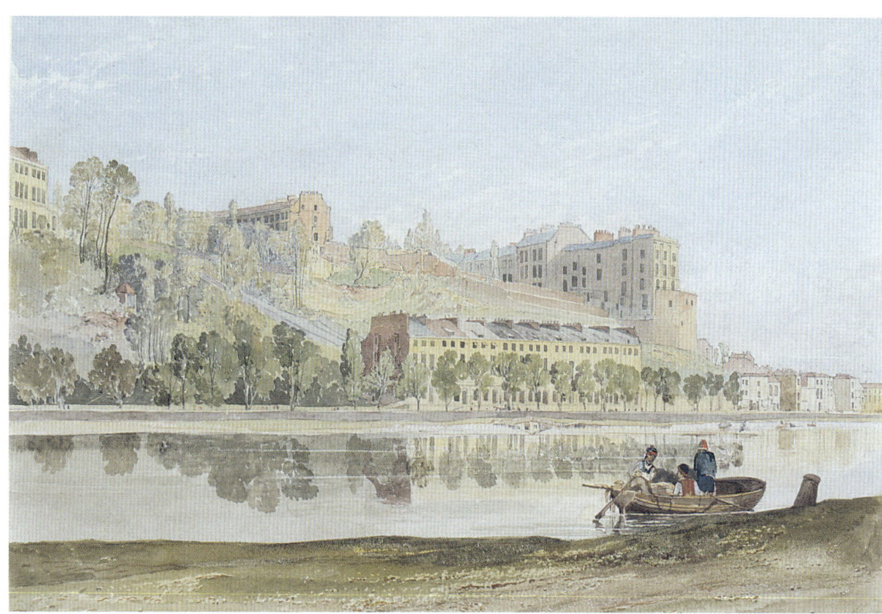

THE ARTISTS

Edward Cashin active 1822-26

Little is known about Edward Cashin apart from a contemporary description of him in 1826 as a shy young Irishman. His work is unknown outside the collections of Bristol antiquaries and his earliest drawing, in the style of O'Neill, is of a house in Broad Street in 1822. He made fifty drawings for Braikenridge between 1823 and 1826 but after that nothing is heard of him. Perhaps he died young. His minutely detailed watercolours have been compared with the seventeenth-century Dutch artist Jan van der Heyden and are among the most attractive in the Braikenridge Collection. Cashin was fascinated with the texture of cobblestones, crumbling walls and tiled roofs. He delighted in abrupt contrasts of light and shade and often animated his drawings with children playing or small dogs padding through Bristol's streets.

Plates: 7, 12, 30, 39, 45, 55, 59, 86, 95, back cover.

George William Delamotte active 1822-1831

George William Delamotte was working in Bristol from 1822 to 1831 but nothing else is known about him. He made only twenty-six drawings for Braikenridge, mainly of street scenes, from July 1824 until the autumn of 1825. Braikenridge gave his Christian names as George William and sometimes spelt his surname De la Motte. It is probable that Braikenridge preferred the work of Rowbotham, who first made drawings for the collection in July 1825 and was the better draughtsman, and employed him instead. Delamotte's street scenes often include attractive detail, such as flower-sellers.

It is possible that he was related to the family of watercolour artists and drawing masters who were working at the same time elsewhere in England. William Alfred Delamotte (1775-1863) spent most of his career in Oxford and is the most well known of the three. His brother, George Orleans De La Motte (active 1809-1830), taught at Sandhurst and Reading. Philip Henry Delamotte (1820-1889) was a son of William Alfred and became a Professor at King's College, London.

Plates: 6, 27, 51, 68, 73, 83.

Samuel Jackson 1794-1869

More is known about Samuel Jackson than the other artists in this book and he has been the subject of a separate Museum publication, *The Bristol Landscape*, where a full account of his life and work can be found. He spent his entire life in Bristol and was born and buried there. He first worked for his father, who had been an accountant and then a dry-salter, and who perhaps opposed his son working as an artist. Jackson was a professional artist by 1822, probably after the death of his father.

Jackson made fewer than thirty watercolours for Braikenridge's extra-illustrations to Barrett but there were many more in his collection, often of the scenery on the outskirts of Bristol or along the river or harbour. He was primarily a landscape watercolourist, although some oils are known; his best work was made in the 1820s and forms an important part of the achievement of the Bristol School of Artists. He became a prosperous and busy drawing master, he kept in touch with the younger generation of artists and was a respected member of Bristol's cultural life. He was also a lifelong friend of Francis Danby (1793-1861) and his earliest watercolours, when they worked together, can be confused with Danby's. He also participated in the group's evening drawing parties and made monochrome wash drawings of imaginary landscapes.

Jackson exhibited regularly in London at the Old Water-Colour Society, including large and romantic compositions in the 1820s.

Their elaborate technique, with much sponging and scratching-out of the pigment, are in constrast to the crisp washes of his Bristol landscapes. Many of the figure groups in the early landscapes were taken from WH Pyne's *Microcosm* (1806) which was published for the use of artists. In 1827 he visited the West Indies and he travelled in Wales, northern England and a little in Scotland. Later in life, two visits to Switzerland dominated his subject matter. His son was the landscape and marine painter Samuel Phillips Jackson (1830-1904).
Plates: 3, 4, 56, 60, 64.

James Johnson 1802/3-1834

James Johnson was the son of a publican at Downend, a village outside Bristol. His earliest dated drawing is 1819 but it is not until 1821 that more examples of his work are known. In a few years, Johnson developed from being a precise but unexceptional recorder into a fine architectural draughtsman and watercolourist. There are nearly fifty of his drawings in the Braikenridge Collection. He exhibited in London at the Royal Academy and the British Institution but today only a small number of his oil paintings are known and they vary in quality. The Tate Gallery has the only large romantic landscape firmly attributed to him: 'The Tranquil Lake: Sunset Seen through a Ruined Abbey'.

Johnson participated in the evening sketching groups where Bristol School artists and amateurs socialised and sketched romantic compositions in sepia. In common with the other artists, he could find patrons in Bristol for his local topographical drawings but few for large romantic landscapes in oil. Consequently, in the autumn of 1825 he moved to London. Some of Johnson's prices are recorded as a result of this move, as when he left Bristol he sold his stock of drawings. Braikenridge paid £5 for two; they were a view of Bristol from Brandon Hill and an unfinished interior of Bristol Cathedral, both watercolours of 1825. Eight earlier ones were offered for a total of £10. Johnson returned to Bristol by the end of 1826 but was still unable to make a living from selling his work so moved to Bath and taught drawing. Johnson's contemporaries in Bristol spoke highly of him, both for his talent and his gentle character, but he was also 'melancholy'. This led to a recurring illness. Towards the end of his life he seems to have visited the West Indies with a brother who was a ship's captain. His illness returned afterwards and in the summer of 1834, at the age of 31, he threw himself from a window whilst under confinement in Bath.
Plates: 10, 19, 20, 29, 31, 44, 65, 67, 85, 105.

Hugh O'Neill 1784-1824

Braikenridge's account of the life of Hugh O'Neill is in Bristol Central Reference Library and includes the portrait of him illustrated here. The artist is unknown. It is a rare print, and was perhaps never published. O'Neill was born in London, the son of Jeremiah O'Neill, an architect. He received encouragement from Dr Monro, mentor of many young topographical and landscape artists, and became a drawing master at Oxford. Some of his early drawings are in the Ashmolean Museum. He moved briefly to Edinburgh and then to Bath where he taught from 1813 to 1820. He then moved to Bristol where he immediately met Braikenridge by 'chance'. O'Neill's talents as an antiquarian draughtsman were perfectly suited to Braikenridge's project and he worked almost exclusively for him, usually in monochrome wash.

In 1822 O'Neill made a design for a suspension bridge across the Avon at Clifton, which he copied for Braikenridge, and he also seems to have undertaken architectural work. In all, he made 441 drawings for the collection.

Braikenridge wrote of him after his death that 'His manners were very gentlemanly and his taste for the fine arts very correct and conspicuous' but also complained of his 'indolent and irregular habits, in which he allowed himself great indulgence' and which resulted in debts. However, there was no doubting the quality of his work: 'The genius of Mr. Hugh O'Neill whose truth and beauty of architectural outline and landscape perspective was the most faithful that can be conceived and executed with amazing facility'. 106

Plates: title page, 8, 9, 13, 23, 25, 26, 32, 33, 35, 38, 41, 42, 43, 46, 47, 48, 54, 66, 72, 74, 76, 79, 81, 82, 88, 91, 93, 99, 102.

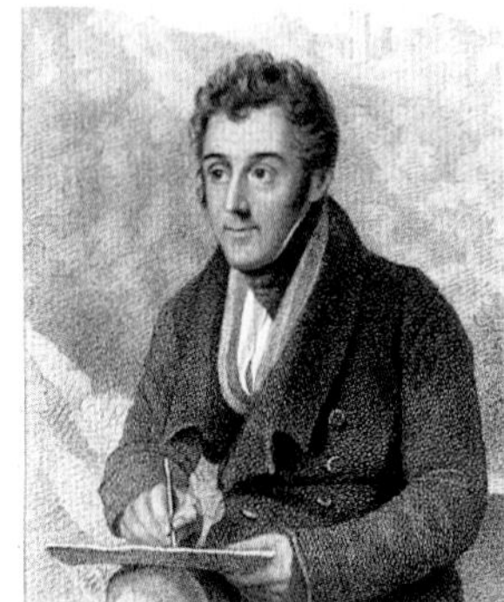

***Hugh O'Neill* c. 1820**

Thomas Leeson Rowbotham 1782-1853

Thomas Leeson Rowbotham was born in Bath in 1782. His date of birth has previously always been given as 1783 but recent research by a descendant has confirmed his dates as 1782-1853. He has also formerly been listed as Thomas Leeson Scarse Rowbotham, although Braikenridge referred to him as Thomas Scrase Rowbotham in 1826; however, all primary sources for his life give his Christian names as Thomas Leeson only. Mysteriously, one small oil painting of 1803 in the Museum's collection is signed T.LS. Rowbotham.

In 1811 he was working in Bath as a teacher of marine painting, cottage figures and landscape. He moved to Dublin soon after but by 1825 had settled in Bristol where he remained for a decade. He lived at various addresses in the city working as a drawing master, including teaching Braikenridge's daughters. In 1828 he lived at 3 Somerset Street, Kingsdown, and the elevated view of the city may have inspired him to begin the panoramas, which seem to have been the last work he made for Braikenridge. Rowbotham's work is little known outside the Braikenridge collection. He made 258 watercolours for the Bristol collection and many of the preliminary pencil drawings, with notations, survive in a local private collection. There are also about 100 drawings of Brislington and a few romantic sepia drawings.

In 1832 and 1833 lithographs were made after his drawings of the 1831 Bristol Riots. He then moved to London where he taught at the Royal Naval School, New Cross, Lewisham. He died in Camberwell in 1853. He wrote *The art of sketching from nature* and, with his son, *The Art of Landscape Painting in Water Colours*. Both were reprinted many times and by 1852 were in their 20th and 8th editions respectively. The work of his son, the watercolourist Thomas Charles Leeson Rowbotham (1823-1875), is rather better known than his own. Father and son are often listed as Rowbotham senior and junior.

Plates: front cover, 2, 5, 11, 14, 15, 16, 17, 18, 21, 22, 24, 28, 34, 36, 37, 40, 49, 50, 52, 53, 57, 58, 61, 62, 63, 69, 70, 71, 75, 77, 78, 80, 84, 87, 89, 90, 92, 94, 96, 97, 98, 100, 101, 103, 104, 108, 109.

LIST OF ILLUSTRATIONS

Unless otherwise stated, all works are part of the bequest by Jerdone Braikenridge of his father's collection to the City of Bristol, 1908. The alpha-numeric numbers are Bristol Museums & Art Gallery inventory numbers.

58 *The Cathedral and College Green from Great George Street* 1827 Thomas L Rowbotham M2538
59 *St George's Church, Great George Street* 1824 Edward Cashin M2554
60 *View of Bristol from below the Royal Fort, Tyndall's Park, with Evan Baillie's house* 1825 Samuel Jackson M3416
61 *The steps connecting Griffin Lane and Church Lane* 1828 Thomas L Rowbotham M2563
62 *St Michael's Hill* 1828 Thomas L Rowbotham M2566
63 *View from the top of Lodge Street* 1826 Thomas L Rowbotham M2570
64 *The Red Lodge from Lodge Street* 1824 Samuel Jackson M2571
65 *Steep Street* 1822 James Johnson M2586
66 *The City School (Queen Elizabeth's Hospital) in Christmas Street* 1820 Hugh O'Neill M2572
67 *The White Lodge, seen from the garden of the City School (Queen Elizabeth's Hospital) at the St Bartholomew's in Christmas Street* 1824 James Johnson M2559
68 *Queen Street (later Christmas Steps)* 1825 George W Delamotte M2560
69 *Lower Maudlin Lane* 1826 Thomas L Rowbotham M2841
70 *Montague Street and houses on Kingsdown* 1826 Thomas L Rowbotham M2837
71 *Spring Hill from King Square* 1828 Thomas L Rowbotham M2828
72 *A house behind Baldwin Street* 1823 Hugh O'Neill M2218
73 *Baldwin Street* 1824 George W Delamotte M2299
74 *Houses on Bristol Back near the end of King Street* 1823 Hugh O'Neill M2236
75 *The Old Custom House on Bristol Back* 1825 Thomas L Rowbotham M2238
76 *The Rackhay, off Back Street* 1821 Hugh O'Neill M2243
77 *King Street 1825* Thomas L Rowbotham M2509
78 *A Passage off Marsh Street* 1827 Thomas L Rowbotham M2513
79 *Marsh Street* 1823 Hugh O'Neill M2512
80 *Prince Street* 1826 Thomas L Rowbotham M2506
81 *Bristol Bridge* 1823 Hugh O'Neill M2962
82 *The Counterslip* 1820 Hugh O'Neill M2163
83 *The Neptune, Church Lane, near Temple Church* 1825 George W Delamotte M2170
84 *Temple Street* 1828 Thomas L Rowbotham M2110
85 *The Weavers' Chapel, Temple Church* 1828 James Johnson M2112
86 *Burton's Almshouses, Long Row* 1824 Edward Cashin M2088
87 *St Mary Redcliffe seen from Redcliffe Street* 1828 Thomas L Rowbotham M1932
88 *The Red Lion Inn, Redcliffe Street* 1823 Hugh O'Neill M2038
89 *Chimney-piece at 28 Redcliffe Street* 1825 Thomas L Rowbotham M2098
90 *St Mary Redcliffe Church from the north-east* 1826 Thomas L Rowbotham M1937
91 *Redcliffe Hill with the Shot Tower* 1822 Hugh O'Neill M2045
92 *Hill's Bridge on the Bath Road* 1826 Thomas L Rowbotham M3414
93 *Glasshouses in St Philip's* 1821 Hugh O'Neill M2777
94 *The Floating Harbour from Redcliffe Back Ferry* 1826 Thomas L Rowbotham K2224
95 *Bathurst Basin* 1825 Edward Cashin M2103
96 *Eastern Wapping Dock* 1826 Thomas L Rowbotham M2951
97 *Eastern Wapping Dock with the launch of the barque* Avon *1826* Thomas L. Rowbotham M2944
98 *Western Wapping Dock* 1826 Thomas L Rowbotham M2945
99 *The Floating Harbour, looking towards St Mary Redcliffe and the back of the New Gaol* 1822 Hugh O'Neill M3385
100 *The Butts, near Tombs' Dock* 1825 Thomas L Rowbotham M2923
101 *The Quay, looking north, with the Old Corn Exchange* 1825 Thomas L Rowbotham M2920
102 *Brandon Hill and the Limekiln Dock* 1822 Hugh O'Neill M2961
103 *Hilhouse's New Dockyard* 1826 Thomas L Rowbotham M2939
104 *The Overfall Dam* 1827 Thomas L Rowbotham M2931
105 *The Paragon, Windsor Terrace and St Vincent's Parade* 1823 James Johnson M2964
106 *Portrait of Hugh O'Neill* c.1820 stipple engraving Bristol Central Reference Library, Braikenridge Collection, XXVI, ii, 112
107 *Portrait of TL Rowbotham* c.1825 Nathan Cooper Branwhite Purchased with the assistance of the Friends of Bristol Art Gallery, 1989. K5429
108 *Panoramic view of Bristol from Pile Hill, Totterdown* c.1829 Thomas L Rowbotham Mb497
109 *Panoramic view of Bristol from Prior's Hill Fort, Kingsdown* c.1829 Thomas L Rowbotham Mb503

SELECTED BIBLIOGRAPHY

It has not been possible to cite references in a publication of this nature but full details on Braikenridge's life and collections will be found in my thesis, see below. The Braikenridge manuscript catalogues in Bristol Museums & Art Gallery and his collection at Bristol Central Reference Library were the source for much material. In addition, the detail of John Plumley and George Ashmead's superb large-scale map of the city *Plan of the City of Bristol and its Suburbs* (surveyed 1813-1828, published 1829) has enabled the precise location of drawings to be identified.

Aldous, Tony, and Trelawny-Ross, John, *C20: Bristol's Twentieth-Century Buildings*, Bristol, Redcliffe Press for The Architecture Centre, 2000.

Bettey, Joseph, *Bristol Observed: Visitors' impressions of the City from Domesday to The Blitz*, Bristol, Redcliffe Press, 1986.

Bettey, Joseph (ed.), *Historic Churches and Church Life in Bristol,* Bristol, Bristol & Gloucestershire Archaeological Society, 2001.

Brown, Dorothy, *Bristol Castle and the Old Market area*, Bristol, Bristol Visual & Environmental Group, 1977.

Chilcott's Descriptive History of Bristol, Ancient and Modern, or, *A Guide to Bristol, Clifton, and the Hotwells*, Bristol, J Chilcott, 4th ed., circa 1840.

Elkin, Paul, *Images of Maritime Bristol*, Derby, Breedon Books, 1995.

Evans, John, *The New Guide, or Picture of Bristol*, Bristol, 3rd ed., circa 1820.

Gomme, Andor, Jenner, Michael and Little, Bryan, *Bristol: an architectural history*, London, Lund Humphries in association with Bristol & West Building Society, 1979.

Greenacre, Francis, *The Bristol School of Artists; Francis Danby and Painting in Bristol 1810-1840*, Bristol, exhibition catalogue, Bristol City Art Gallery, 1973.

Greenacre, Francis, and Stoddard, Sheena, *The Bristol Landscape; the Watercolours of Samuel Jackson 1794-1869*, City of Bristol Museum & Art Gallery, 1986.

Grey, Irvine, *Antiquaries of Gloucestershire and Bristol,* Gloucester, Alan Sutton Ltd for the Bristol and Gloucestershire Archaeological Society, 1981.

Latimer, John, *Annals of Bristol 1700-1900*, 7 vols, Bristol, 1906.

Little, Bryan, *Churches in Bristol*, Bristol, Redcliffe Press, 1978.

Little, Bryan, *Church Treasures in Bristol*, Bristol, Redcliffe Press, 1979.

Lord, John, and Southam, Jem, *The Floating Harbour; a landscape history of Bristol City Docks*, Bristol, Redcliffe Press, 1983.

Manson, Michael, *Bristol; Beyond the Bridge*, Bristol, Redcliffe Press, 1988.

Mathews' Bristol Directory

Mathews' Bristol Guide, Bristol, J Mathews, 3rd ed., 1815.

Nicholls, JF, and Taylor, John, *Bristol Past and Present*, 3 vols, Bristol, 1881-2.

Priest, Gordon and Cobb, Pamela (eds), *The Fight for Bristol; planning and the growth of public protest*, Bristol, Bristol Civic Society and Redcliffe Press, 1980.

Punter, John V, *Design Control in Bristol 1940-1990*, Bristol, Redcliffe Press, 1990.

Southey, Robert, *Letters from England*, 1807, republished Gloucester, Alan Sutton Ltd., 1984.

Stoddard, Sheena, *George Weare Braikenridge (1775-1856), a Bristol Antiquarian and his Collections*, unpublished M.Litt. thesis, University of Bristol, 1983.

Stoddard, Sheena, *Mr Braikenridge's Brislington*, City of Bristol Museum & Art Gallery, 1981.

Temple Local History Group (Julian Lea-Jones *et al*), *An account of St John's Conduit – Bristol's Medieval Water System*, Bristol, 1984.

Watson, Sally, *Secret Underground Bristol*, Bristol, Bristol Junior Chamber, 1991.

Witt, Cleo, Weeden, Cyril and Schwind, Arlene Palmer, *Bristol Glass*, Bristol, Redcliffe Press, 1984.

The Panoramas

In 1829-30 Thomas L Rowbotham drew four panoramas of Bristol for Braikenridge and two of them are reproduced here. They can be seen as a conclusion to the antiquary's work on recording the topography of his city and he made only minor additions to the collection in later years.

107

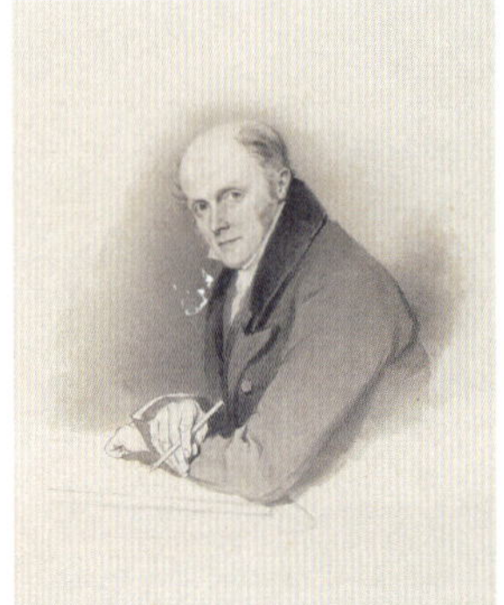

***TL Rowbotham* c.1825**
Nathan Cooper Branwhite

***Panoramic view of Bristol from Pile Hill, Totterdown* c.1829**

This view was drawn from Pile (or Pylle) Hill and today Pylle Hill Crescent commemorates the name. The panorama covers a very wide view, about 220°.

The construction of the Floating Harbour had created new physical boundaries to the city and the area between St Mary Redcliffe and the New Cut was quickly built-up. The drawing is a valuable record of an area which is very different today.

***Panoramic view of Bristol from Prior's Hill Fort, Kingsdown* c.1829**

This panorama is a 180° view of Bristol. It is not, however, drawn from one viewpoint but is a clever compilation of several views. It is taken from the upper rooms or even the roofs of the houses in Somerset Street. Dove Street runs along much of the foreground and if you walk today along its upper section it is possible to envisage this view.

The name Prior's Hill recalls the time when Kingsdown was part of the estates of the medieval Priory of St James. Prior's Hill Fort, on the site of today's Fremantle Square, had been part of the fortifications of the city during the Civil War.

108 ***Panoramic view of Bristol from Pile Hill, Totterdown c.1829***
Thomas L Rowbotham

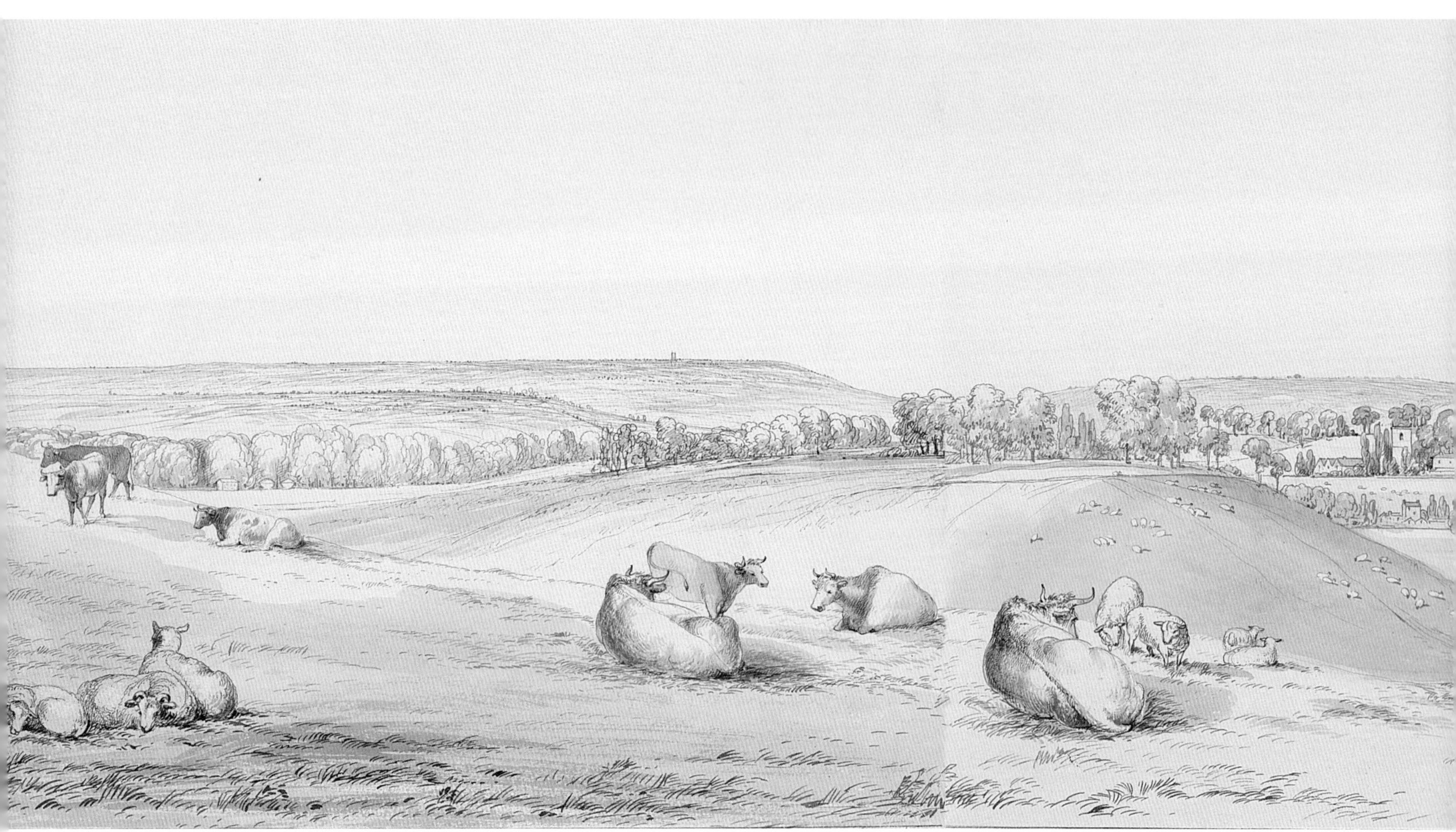

The farm, behind the cow lying down on the left, is in the area of St John's Lane towards Lower Knowle. Dundry Church is on the skyline.

Windmill Hill is in the middle distance. Immediately to its right is the old church of St John the Baptist in Bedminster.

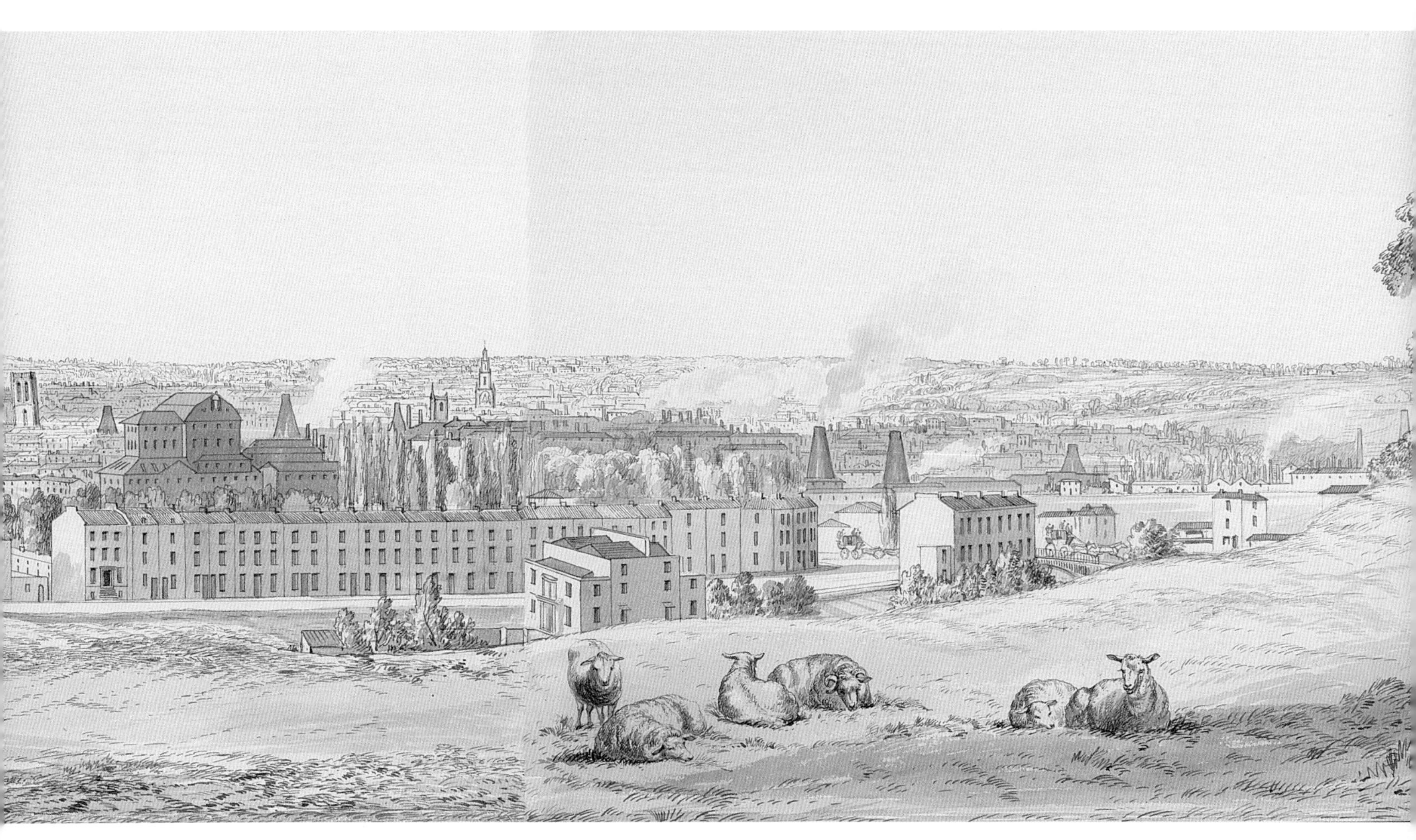

This part of Bristol was dominated by John Hare's Floor-cloth Manufactory next to Temple Meads. Floor cloth was an early form of linoleum. There were several kilns in this area, used either for the manufacture of glass or pottery.
Hill's Bridge, carrying the road to Bath, is seen towards the right. Pile Hill was also known as One Tree Hill and its solitary tree is on the right margin. To Braikenridge's disgust, it was later cut down by a railway engineer.

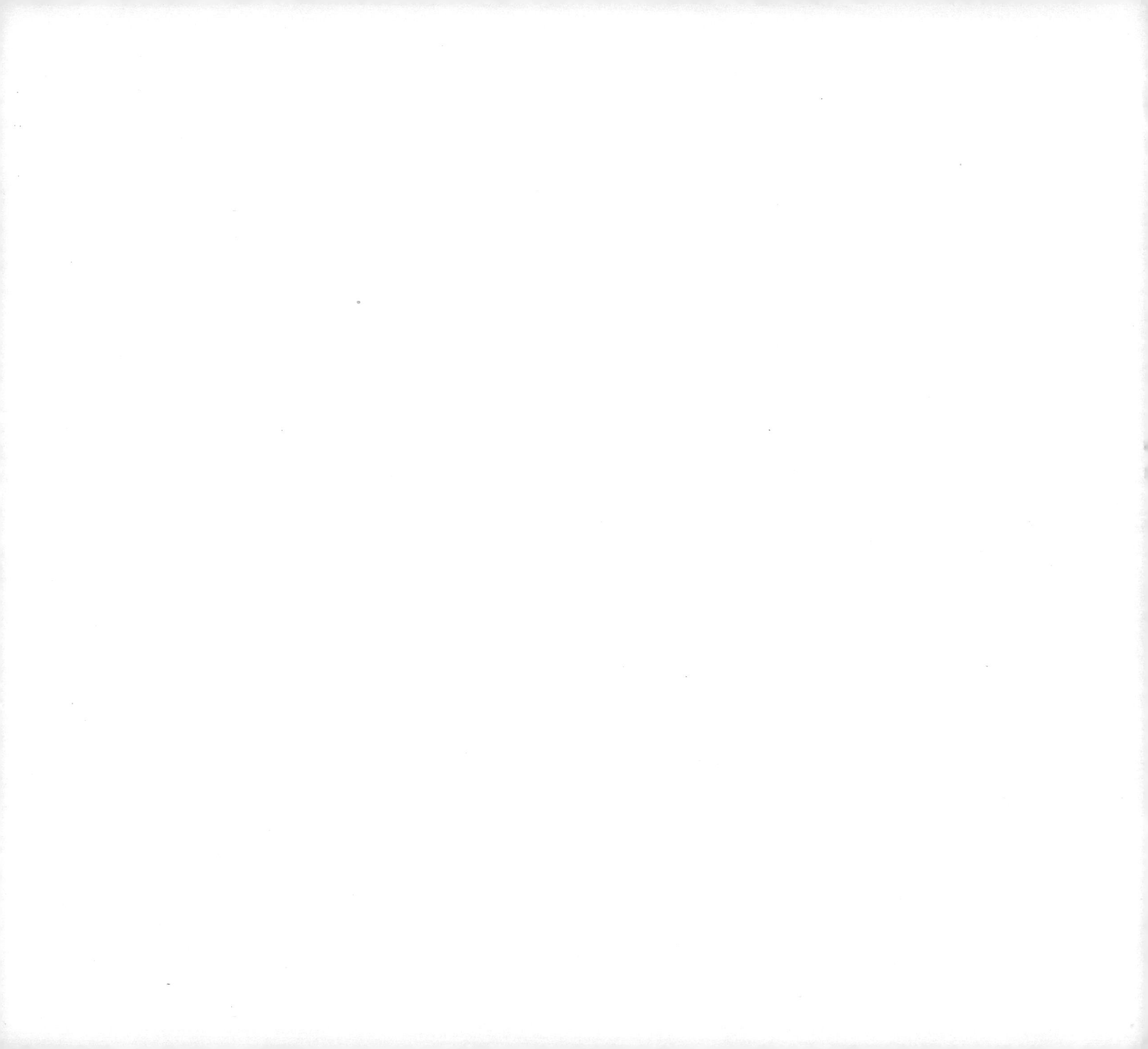

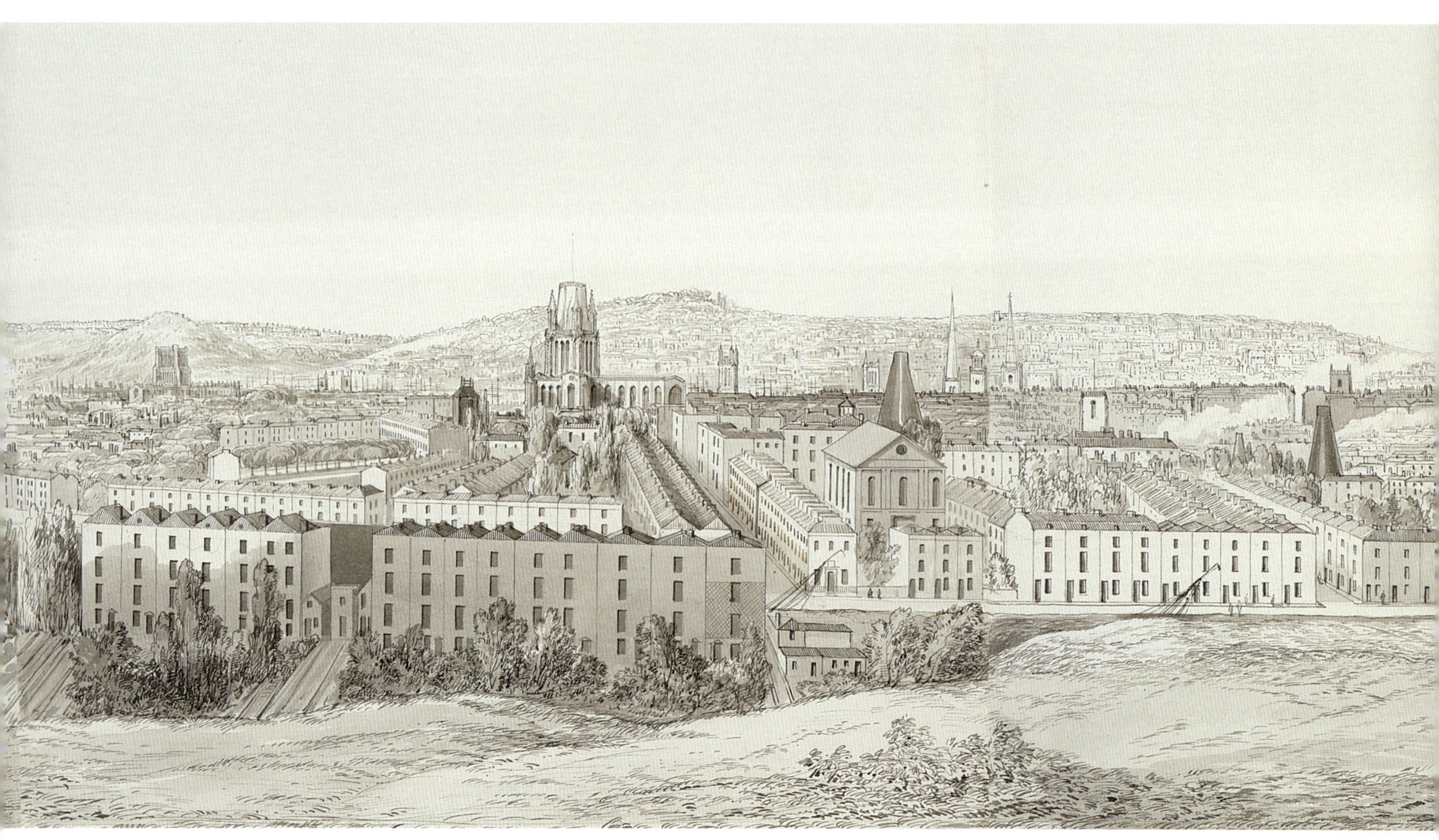

Brandon Hill is on the left horizon, behind the Cathedral. It is strangely denuded of the buildings in Park Street, Great George Street etc. which were there at this time. St Mary Redcliffe is in the centre and the Shot Tower is to its left. Left again is Somerset Square, originally built with an opening giving a prospect into Somersetshire. Langton Street Chapel (Wesleyan) is the tall building in the centre. The kiln above it was the former Prewett Street Glasshouse. Its base is now the restaurant of a hotel and is the only surviving fragment of this once important industry.

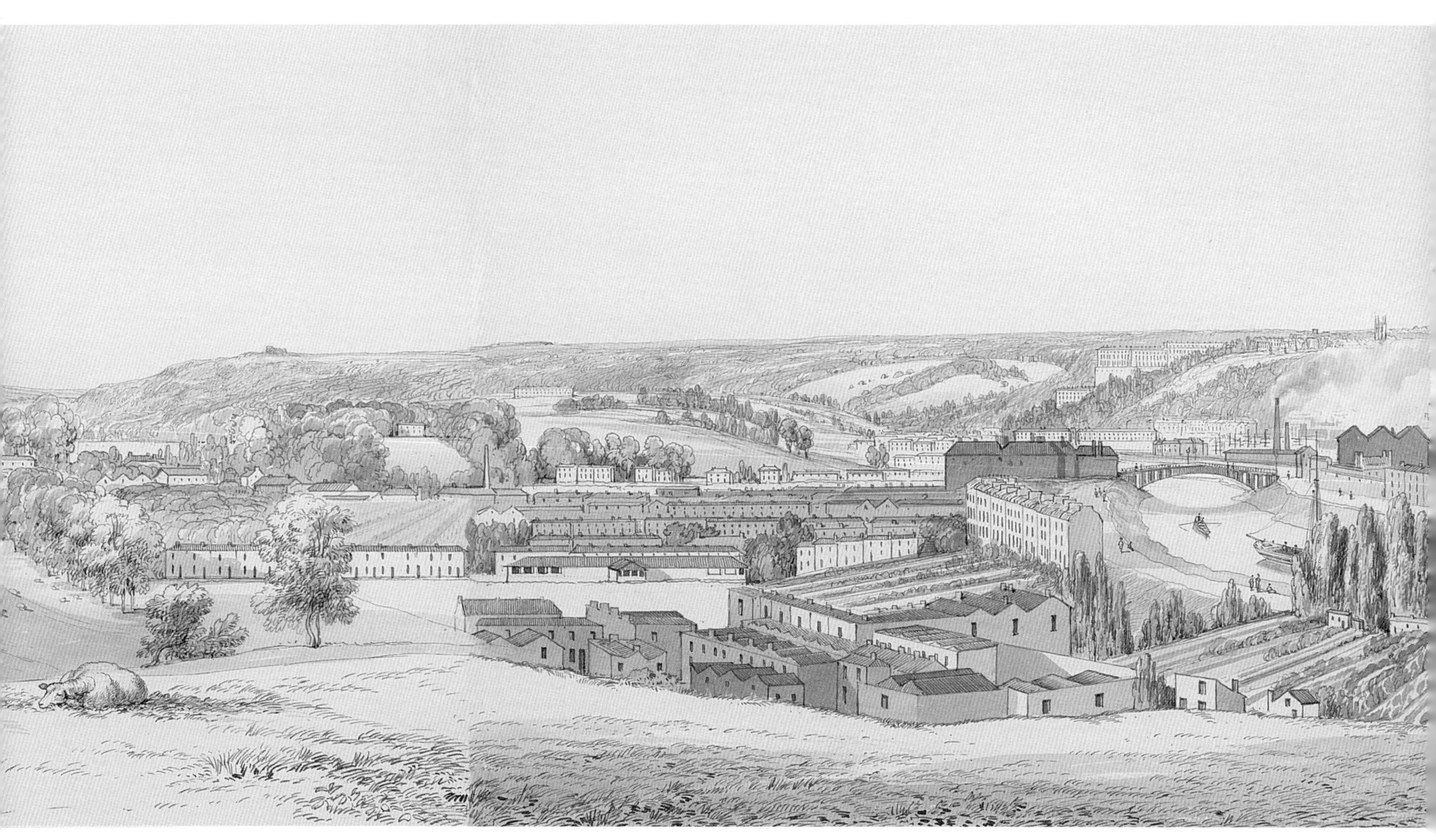

Bedminster dominates this section. The dark buildings to the left of the bridge (also known as Harford's Bridge) is the Bedminster Bridge Brewery. The smoking chimney on the Bristol side is Acraman's Iron Works and the large building with the triple-pitched roof was a former sugar house. Above is Clifton.

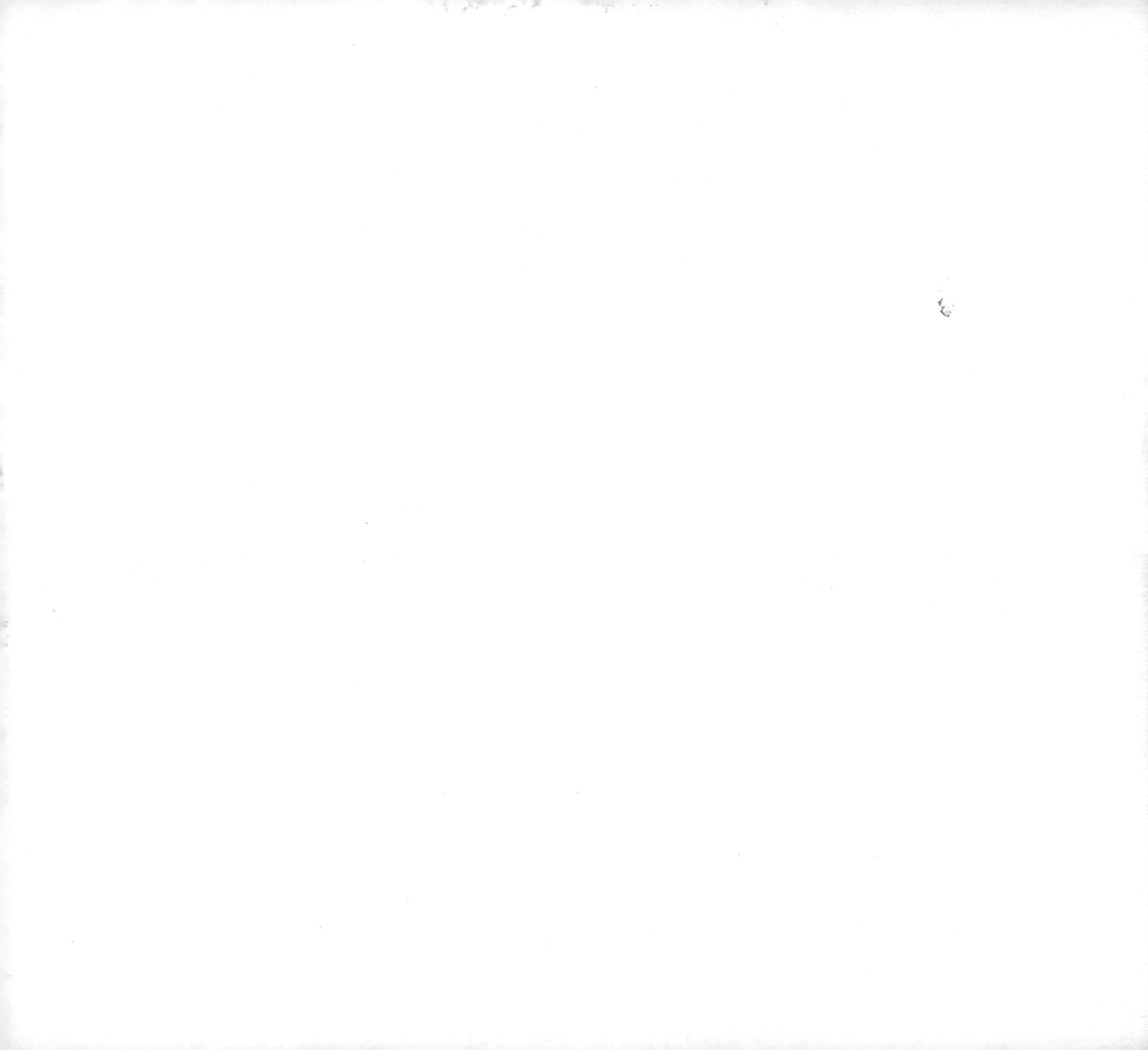

109 ***Panoramic view of Bristol from Prior's Hill Fort, Kingsdown* c.1829**
Thomas L Rowbotham

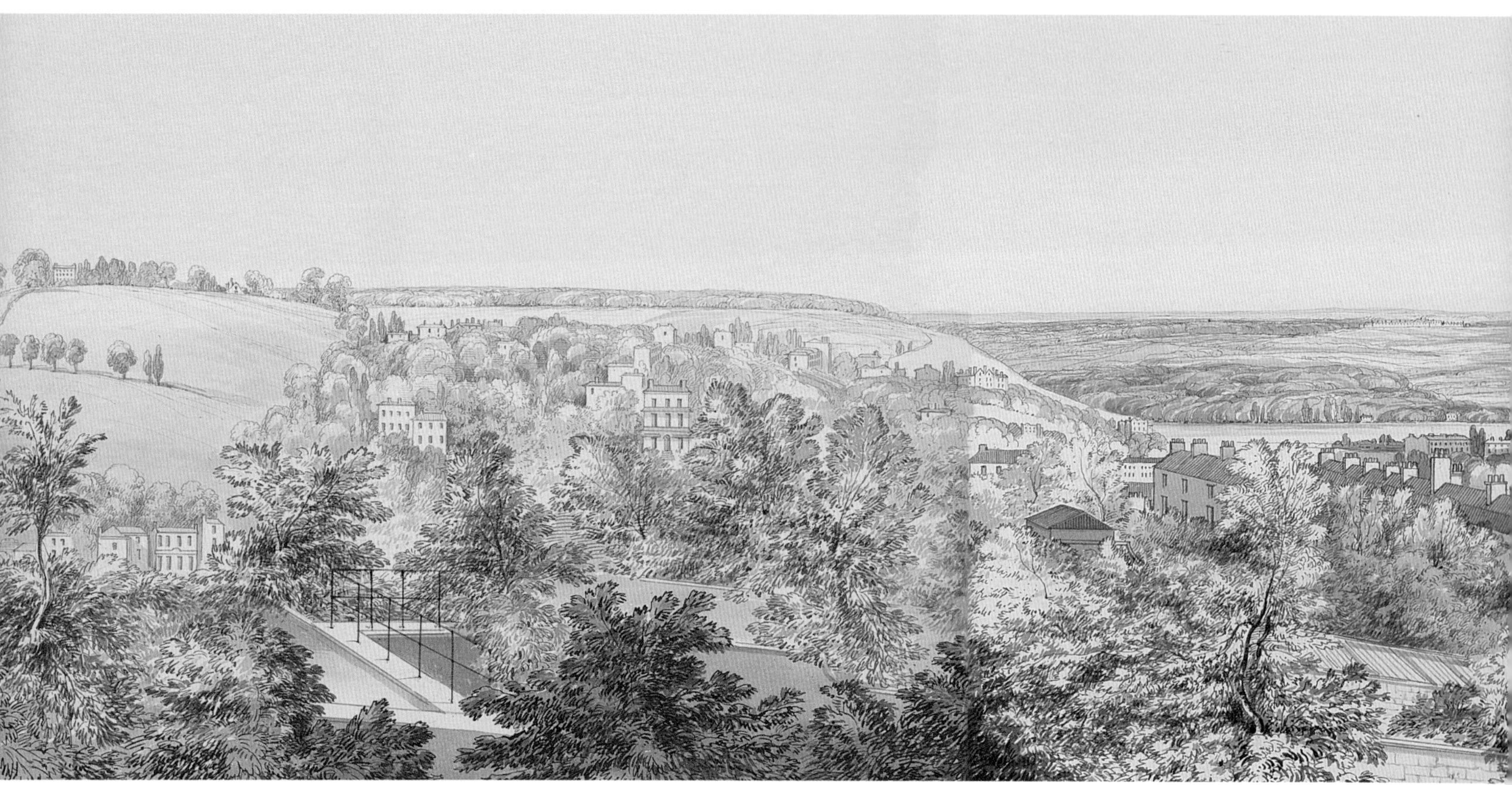

On the left skyline are Ashley Court and the gable of Montpelier Farm in today's St Andrew's. The function of the parapet and rail in the foreground of this section is unknown. Behind, surrounded by trees, are houses in Montpelier.

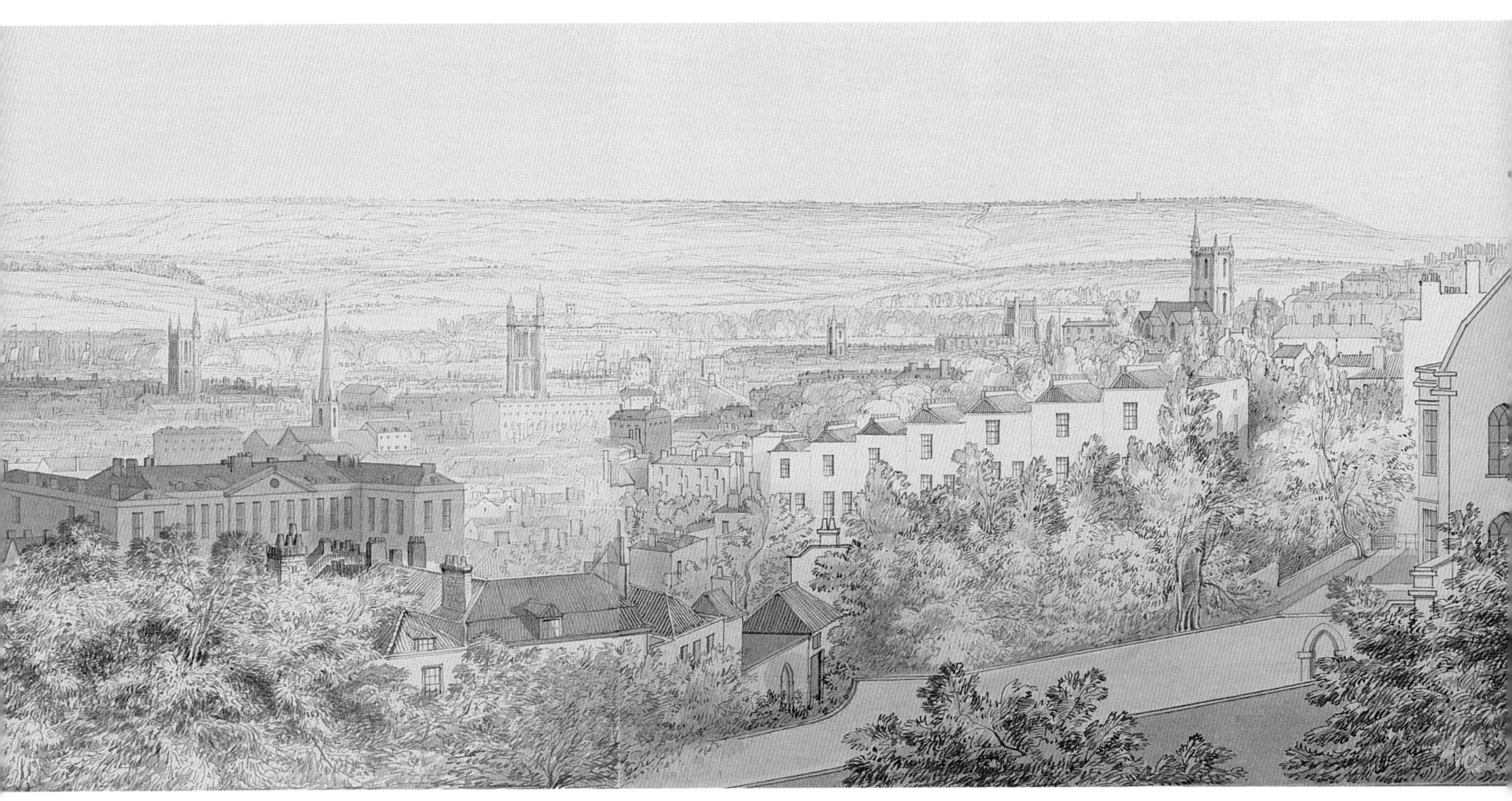

The Infirmary building dominates to the left; the core of the building remains within the Old Building of today's Bristol Royal Infirmary. The tower of St Werburgh's, then in Corn Street, and the spire of St John-on-the-Wall are above it.
The terrace of houses climbing the hill is Marlborough Hill. The church to the right is St Michael's and, above Bedminster Down, Dundry is on the skyline.

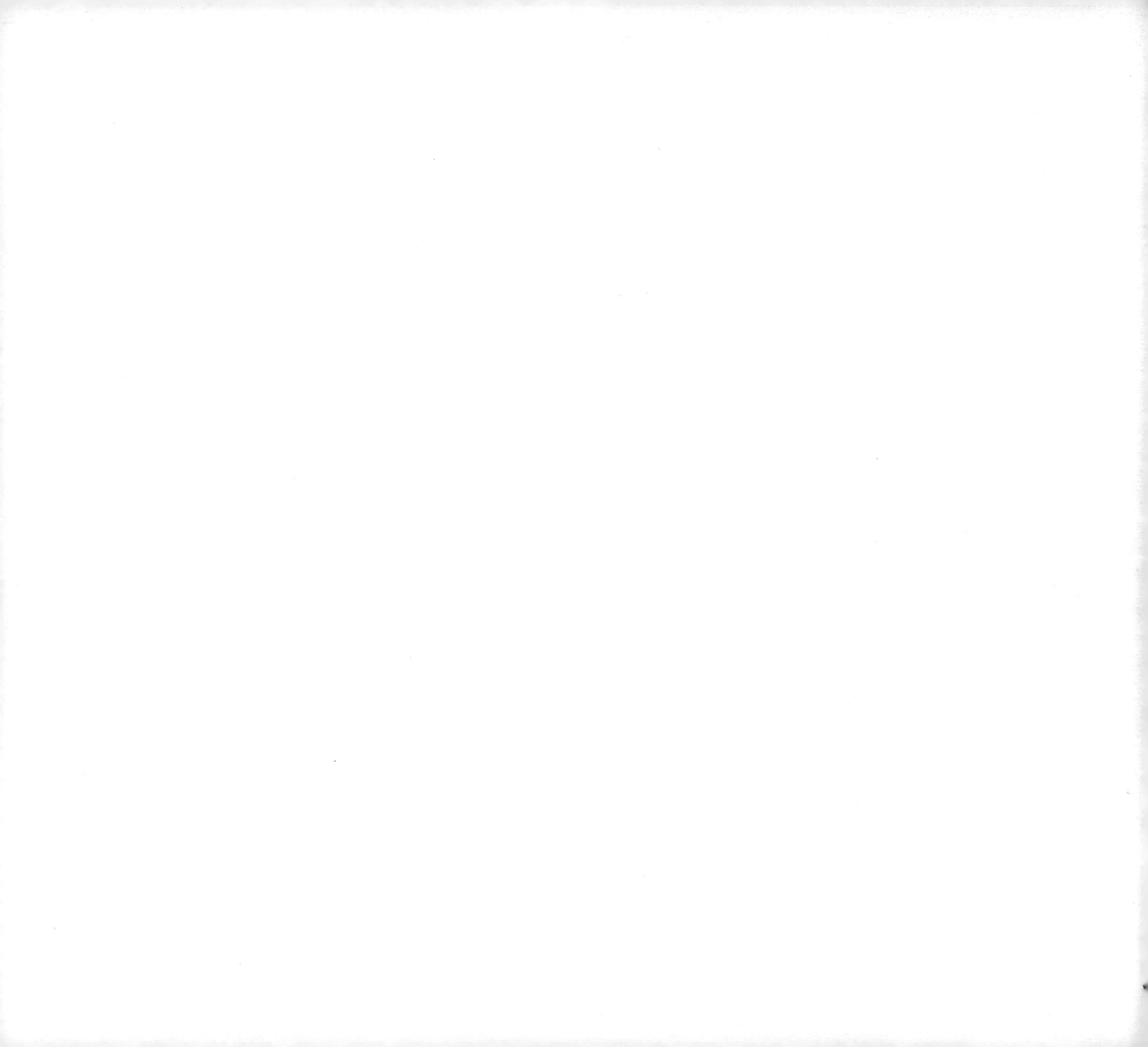

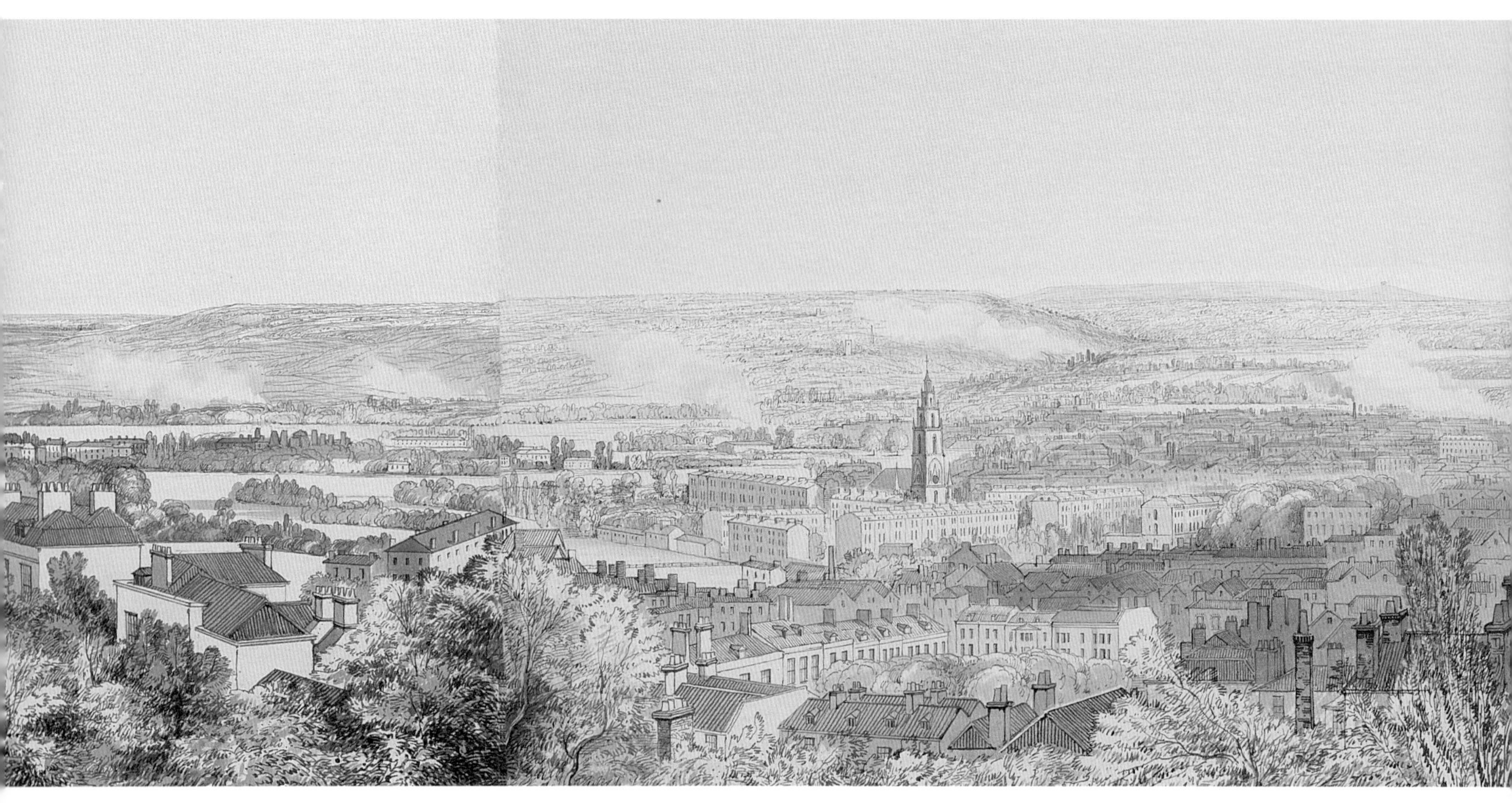

The long building on the left horizon is at Stapleton; it had been used as a prison during the Napoleonic Wars. The smoke beneath it to the right rises from the brass and copper works at Baptist Mills.
Georgian St Paul's was a very fashionable area and its distinctive Gothick church, opened 1794, dominates this section. King Square is in the middle foreground.

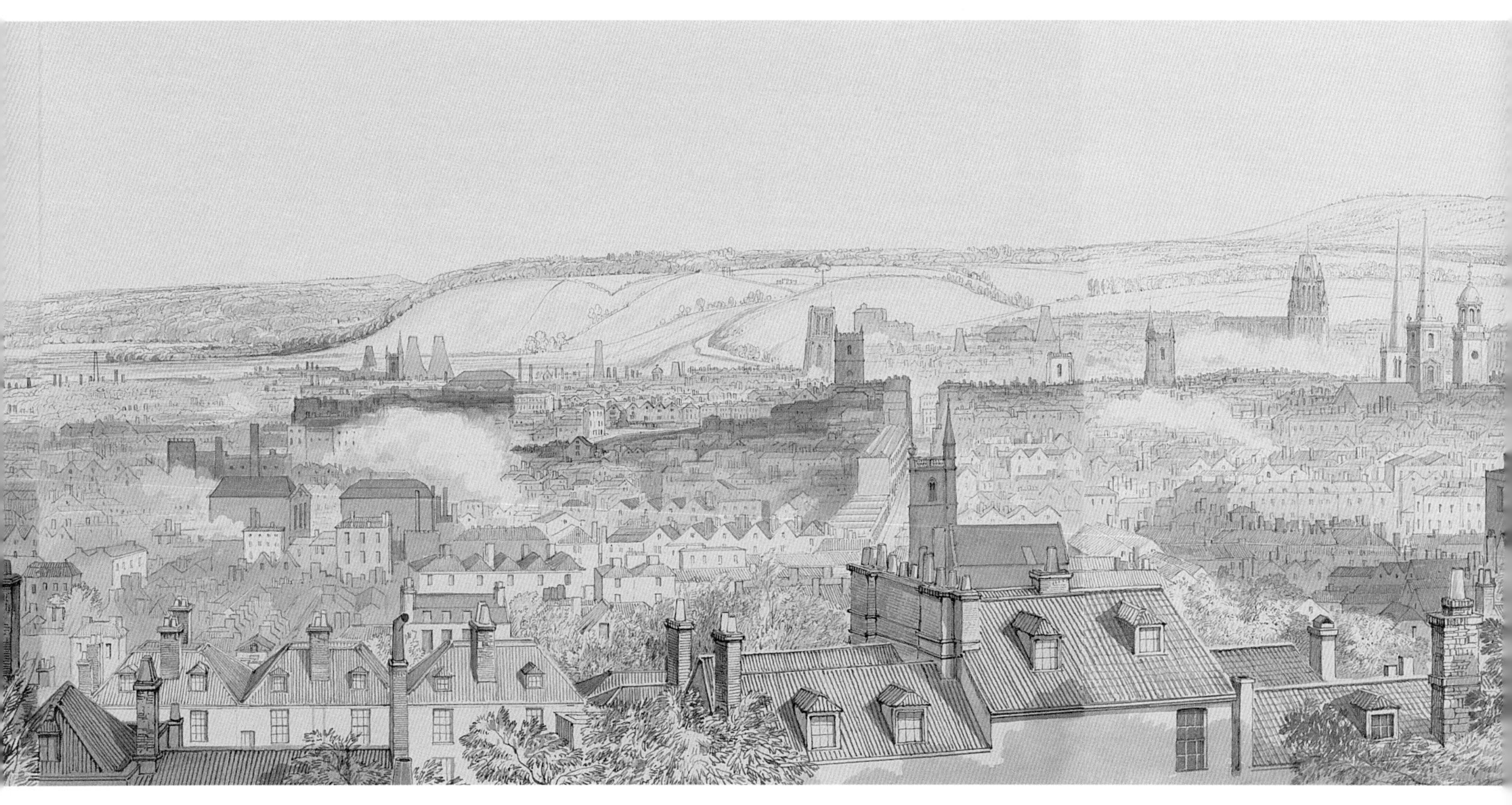

St James's Church is in the middle foreground with Union Street behind. The area to their left is now the Broadmead shopping area and the inner ring-road. The two large buildings beneath the plume of smoke are Nonconformist chapels in Old King Street.